Symbols in Nature

Innocent

&

PURE

Written, Designed & Illustrated By

Timothy J. Culver

Note for Librarians: A cataloguing record for this book is available from Library and Archives Canada at www.collectionscanada.ca/amicus/index-e.html
ISBN 1-4251-0877-6

Offices in Canada, USA, Ireland and UK

Book sales for North America and international:
Trafford Publishing, 6E–2333 Government St.,
Victoria, BC V8T 4P4 CANADA
phone 250 383 6864 (toll-free 1 888 232 4444)
fax 250 383 6804; email to orders@trafford.com
Book sales in Europe:
Trafford Publishing (UK) Limited, 9 Park End Street, 2nd Floor
Oxford, UK OX1 1HH UNITED KINGDOM
phone 44 (0)1865 722 113 (local rate 0845 230 9601)
facsimile 44 (0)1865 722 868; info.uk@trafford.com
Order online at:
trafford.com/06-2635

10 9 8 7 6 5 4 3 2

Review

After reading Timothy J. Culver's book, *Symbols in Nature: Innocent & PURE*, I came away with the warm image of Culver as the guru on a mountaintop, gazing intently at a determined inquisitor, breathless and bloody from climbing the mountain, who asks in great anticipation, "What is the secret of life?" — to which Culver replies, "Nature!"

Culver is to Nature what Keats is to beauty.

The multi-talented poet and illustrator devotes his entire book to Nature, which offers the author a never-ending horizon of its earth, air, water and inhabitants. Culver's words explore them all with his unique blend of poems and dissertations.

His inscrutable searching for Nature's symbols, clues, mysteries and signs reveal the exploratory nature in him as well as the poet. In *To Toil a Seed*, Culver draws the analogy of birth, the toils of life and inevitable death in all mortals as akin to the sowing of a seed, its toils and labors until it has run its course and is considered grown.

The spiritual references are never far from the writer's pen as he refers to the He. His mural is all-encompassing. The subjective viewer will see eclipses, the sun, a rose, a garden, a fly, a spine, a seed, humanity, everything in nature. Even a weed is a revelation to him.

However, the author never assumes the form of a rose, a fly or a weed. It would be an intriguing delight to read in future writings how this beloved friend of nature would don the cloak of personification.

He has a clarity that is not stultified. His style borders on free verse that often begins with a cadence, evaporates in the middle and rises to again ride us on out with a renewed cadence.

At times, he incorporates rhyme with an intended purpose to draw you deeper into his poem. His many works are thought provoking and sensual. I was compelled to return to *Acts of Nature* and *Nature's Voice* several times.

If you want a deeper introspection of the natural world we live in you will find it in the works of Timothy J. Culver. You will never be left stranded on an island of regret.

Jerry Plantz
www.Thepatrioticpoet.

Symbols in Nature

Innocent

&

PURE

That inner voice that speaks the truth through me to you
It's the divine spirit telling us what to do
It's never too late so keep pushing on
Being a carrier of hope will get us all home
Our unique treasure is sown deep within
To push us through this elastic journey
When the search is stretched thin...snap back!

Timothy J. Culver,
Intuition: The Art of Freeing the Mind

Table of Contents

IV. Lasting Impressions...

V. The Sum of Two States

VI. The Final State of Reflection

VII. The Guiding Symbols of Nature's Light

VIII. Crystal Columns

Symbols in Nature Innocent & PURE

Acknowledgments

This book was inspired by a homeless man I encountered while out for dinner one evening. About one week later, I wrote the poem, *Innocent and PURE.* Within the second week I wrote a second poem, *Symbols in Nature*. These two poems gave birth to the substance of this book. The composition, cover design and nature of this book were developed within a two-week period of time as I worked around the clock, driven by inspiration. I cannot explain the motivation to complete this project — it was so unexpected.

I observed the elderly man's physical state of existence and demeanor. He appeared to hold his position of homelessnes with innocence and his state of mind pure, more like a helpless baby. I viewed this man as a symbol in nature, a messenger carrying a unique message saying, "Look closer. Look deeper. See me and hear my voice." I was receptive to him. Speaking to this man was a captivating and humbling experience.

I am very thankful that I was able to grasp this unique moment in time as it generated the inspiration for writing *Symbols in Nature: Innocent & PURE.* This book is a true product of the inspiration that nature offers us daily through her symbols and messages. My hope is that each symbol and message delivered herein will provide the inspiration to consider the state of man's existence in nature and the vast positions we hold while laboring to live.

A special thanks to Marc D. Baldwin, Ph.D, and Arlisa LaShay Culver Felton, MAEd, for their assistance with the coediting of this book.

Symbols in Nature Innocent & PURE

About the Book

Symbols in Nature: Innocent & PURE is a book of poetry that delicately depicts nature in its most innocent and pure state. The creatively expressed symbols bring back a state of inspiring rejuvenation and purification that allows us the opportunity to clearly define our state within nature by realizing the messages that cycle in her voice, "the universal compass."

You will want to experience for yourself the level of truly indescribable inspiration gained from reading this work. With this view of nature, you will be guided toward a new and purposeful direction in your life.

Step into a world that will rejuvenate your mind, body and spirit; share in the author's vision of the world that surrounds us. To know the author's talent is to read his book: *Symbols in Nature: Innocent & PURE.*

"The ultimate driving force
The cycle of symbols in nature's voice
Reveals life's expectations of us
The universal compass"

The author's vivid cycling of symbols in nature is so uniquely descriptive and intertwined! You will find that you will keep this book near, reading time and time again to experience the cycle of the symbols.

Timothy J. Culver, the author of the book *Intuition: The Art of Freeing the Mind*, is one of the most insightful and talented authors of our time!

Symbols in Nature Innocent & PURE

Just a Few Thoughts...

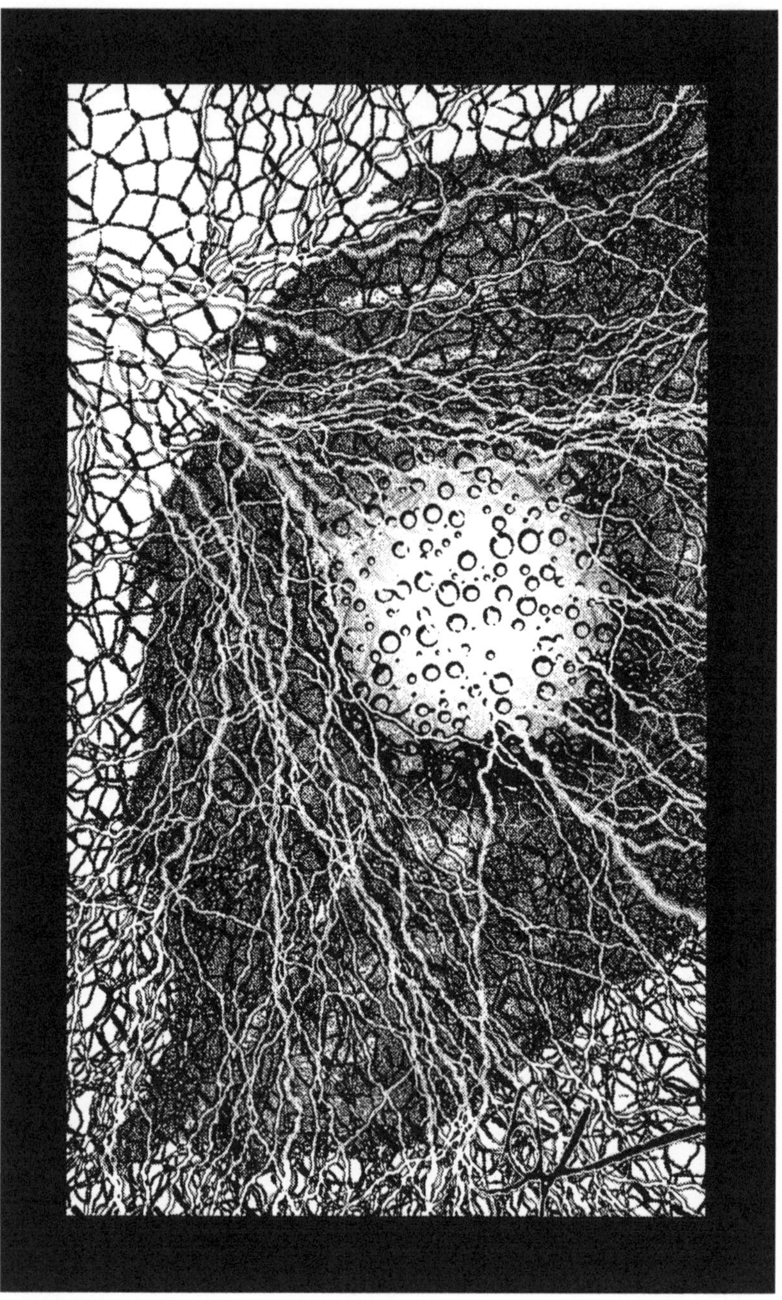

Free Form

Mind over matter
Free to make a matter…
One of good or of bad

The first flight of confidence and transformation in choice
To be or not…

To form an opinion
To form an argument
To form a belief
To form a state of mind
To form an objective
To form a plan
To form a direction
To form a seed
To form a beautiful garden
To form a state of existence
To form a state of freedom
To form a state of life

Nature allows the elements of the earth free form
To be or not to be…

Distractions of Sorts

One thing after another
Murphy's Law in full effect

Not getting a break,
Losing it…

And at the same time, trying to keep it together

Despite of…
In spite of…

Distractions of sorts

Doing all that can be done
Although there is nothing more to do

But to keep it all together, for now,
And a hope to make it through

An overwhelming feeling
Doesn't help anything…

Pessimistic views are only

Distractions of sorts

Inspired by Nature

The natural inclination of a state
Reveals the revelation that is to come by visualizing its reward
Moving forward…

A cycle of symbols in nature called faith

The Mixture

As in the beginning of time
The purest mixture that made up the earth was the beginning of man

Put into a garden
And offered a place of rest
Among the mixture of the elements in all of the earth
So Innocent and PURE in worth
Was reflected in her state of beauty
And in the state of her fruit so plenty

Set free in the garden to eat and to rest
And given the highest name among all of nature
Told never the forbidden fruit to taste
The symbol of guidance to maintain its very state...
Avoid the mixture of the evil with the good
Still, the forbidden fruit man ate
The symbol that consequence is GREAT!
A universal message when dealing with choice

Began the cycle of symbols in nature's voice

The Forces of Nature

The interaction of earth's substantial elements
Compelling to interposition each individual case
The unique energy projected from their varying in natures
A natural competition to form the definite positions of their state

The free form of a compulsive and intervening hand
The deliverer of a mishap to the challenger of its will — to stand
The placement of a freak in nature to hold its inevitable consequence — in hand
Forced to trace the face of each compounding circumstance

A war of spirits, the fight to deliver life eternally and beyond all restrictive natures attacking individual free form of fruit to breed…

The intertwining of generations that feed good seed
Chased by generations of entangling and devouring weed

The cycle of symbols in nature that describes the challenge of our daily walk through life and nature

About the Author

Timothy J. Culver, the second of six children, was born in Newark, N.J., in 1964, to Mrs. Irie Delle (Hogans) Culver and the late Mr. Otis Lee Culver.

He grew up in Abbeville, Ala., where he graduated from high school in 1983. Upon receiving an academic tuition scholarship, he attended Jacksonville State University in Alabama, where he received a BA in Art and Anthropology. He became a member of Alpha Phi Alpha Fraternity, Inc.

Within three years of obtaining his BA, he graduated from Troy State University in Alabama with an MS Fds. Ed. degree in Education and Art. He joined Kappa Delta Pi, an international honors society in education, and was recruited by the Florida Department of Education.

In Florida, he taught at the middle school, high school, and post-secondary levels. His teaching repertoire ranged from drawing fundamentals to advanced design, creative photography, and three-dimensional modeling and animation. He coached football, track and field, and sponsored such clubs as Interact and Art.

He began writing and illustrating while attending Jacksonville State University, where he wrote two books that were adopted into the university's student works permanent collection. As a professional graphic artist, his work ranges from the traditional visual arts to new media design.

He served 17 years in the United States Air Force Reserve and is a veteran of Operation Enduring Freedom.

Mr. Culver is the founder, president and CEO of Making It Personal 4 U Productions, Inc. The company was formed to embrace the creative spirit of others by promoting arts in education and lifestyle. The services provided include scholarships, unique arts information, artist promotion and networking on a global level.

The Embracing Your Creative Spirit Cancer Foundation was also formed by Mr. Culver. The mission of this not-for-profit organization is to provide alternative financial support to cancer victims and their families.

Copyright © 2007 Timothy J. Culver
Making It Personal 4 U Productions, Inc.

The Rules of Composition

Symbols in Nature

The ultimate driving force
The cycle of symbols in nature's voice
Reveals life's expectations of us
The universal compass

They give guidance to those of us who listen
And who will pay close attention
To yield to the signs that say to "hear" nature's voice
Enter into the core of a seed
And to exit its shell anew…
Having knowledge and wisdom indeed
With each new birth gives a seed of life
And as it lives will surely have some strife

The symbols in nature from the mother earth

A seed must be toiled in the dirt and drenched with the tears of nature
The cost for the bearing of fruit will require giving labor
If the core of a fruit is not nurtured it will eventually become hollow
And after the cycle of giving birth a death will surely follow

For, the core of a seed possesses the truth of its nature
It harvests numerous signals to enhance our search for life
A reviving and revolving cycle with each new birth, death and strife
Always goes back into the simplicity of the dirt to sow
The symbols that a seed carries are planted just below

The symbols in nature from the mother earth

Innocent and PURE...

The state from the very beginning
A most valuable state of existence
We were all once Innocent and PURE...
Or, were we?

What is the nature of a seed?
Are all seed receptive to the nature of a pure state?

Or, does the earth itself clean and transform all seed into the state of purity by embracing it and nurturing the state of its existence...just as one would a newly born baby?

For, the nutrients of the earth do nurture the seed
By providing it a home, a place to take root and yet...
Allowing it to break the surface to stand uniquely among all others
To be separate and independent
Having its own characteristics
Bearing its own fruit...

The reflection of innocence and purity is cycled in the state of human existence
The repetition and revolving of a state
Designed by the majestic power of nature
To cleanse the state of all our seed

We're all given the opportunity to bear fruit
An opportunity — to give a home of nurturing
To provide nutrients in which to take root
To embrace a seed that has a state of being...

A most valuable state of existence
The state from the very beginning...

Innocent and PURE...

The Call to Labor

No element of the earth is without labor
A chore, defined from the beginning of time
Each being unique in its own favor

So shall it be done, from now until the end, and life on this earth has passed
All of nature must answer the call to labor
The constant reminder of what He has asked…

The call to labor is an honor and a precious gift for life eternal

The Bridge

The bridge runs from here to there
Raised by columns on which hard pillars rest
Mended together they find their preserved strength
Appear delicate from a distance

Glazed from the mist of morning
Towers of light posts dress its edges
And travel like mirrored images,
Reflections of crystals

The sky pads its position
To stand courageously and project each layered surface
Still appearing delicate, it bears its ground
Among all other things around

A beautiful vision of design when blended with nature
Hovering above its liquid twin
Always makes the travel seem so exciting
Looking up to see its strength revealed

Whose hands built the bridge described?

And They Were Naked...

The state of being naked
Is to be known naked...

So it was from the beginning of time
That the mother earth was naked and raw
Carrying all its elements among the universe, oh so pure!
And there was no one but the He who saw

For as much in naked beauty, the earth did sit
Still and void...
Was not merely enough for the He to compensate His vision of it
So up from the earth — the soil He did toil

The clay was rich with nutrients
Possessed by the mother earth,
But, in it was needed the power of the He
So He gave to it His word

And on a day so grand to begin
Chose to create man from the earth — He raised up the dirt
And formed it into a symbol
Filling it with His breath, His worth

And from the breast of this symbol He called man
He took a rib and made it equal there
To complete the beautification of His symbols to make a pair
He called the second, a woman and adorned her with a composition fair
And told them...

Not the fruit to bear
They were at this time…
Innocent and PURE

And on one day a fruit they did bear
Tasting of the tempting and forbidden ground to fall
Only to learn that they were naked
When the Waking Giant called

To question why — the fruit does take
The symbol of an apple they ate?
Reveals the bearing of life from a tree, with seed
Holding life in the purest state

The fruit of life so Innocent and PURE
Was taken away by the two to eat
They shared the fruit of their nature in the garden dear
And brought forth a new seed with a core to nurture

Now, after sowing into the purest state of the clay to coil
Their seed combined formed the energy of a new life
Brought about the labors of the earth to toil
To bear their fruit and the burdens of its strife

So it was from the beginning of time
He gave chores for them to own and endure
A reminder of their call to labor
To earn back the state of pure

And they were naked…

The Waking Giant

What a sound!
His call can be heard in the universe
Around the earth,
The Waking Giant

He travels around the mother earth with a movement so natural and so swift
A sure symbol that her elements are in need of His merciful and precious gift

For all of the earth's elements know to answer — when He calls
And in His passing, each, no doubt, will humbly take a bow

To thank Him for the gifts He leaves granting the opportunity to be freed
The greatest reverence for the opportunity to universally labor and nurture a seed

Amazingly enough, His entrance call is the storm
A symbol of transformation through the stages of spiritual growth
Required for the soul of a seed to take its purest form

And, after the storm, the earth settles to a calmer state of weather
A symbol in nature each time He wakes us
Saying, "the cycle of life will soon get better"

To Toil a Seed

When a seed is sown into the mother earth,
It yields one's labor by the molding of the dirt
But, the mere nature of its evolution would not nearly be known
Until it has run its course and is considered to be grown

For each new seed that is sown is great
Requires the toiling of the earth around and about it
By the guiding hands of a laboring magistrate
To bring forth the unique nature within its core
Means to nurture it, to praise it, and raise it to develop even more
And, if it is given the right attention,
Would exceed expectations beyond what could be mentioned

To toil a seed — to believe in its potential for all the right reasons
To labor through each storm and calm of each new season

A unique call to labor and a course for learning life's lessons

The seed of a child is sown into its mother
Yielding one's labor through its birth and life on earth
But, the mere nature of its development would not nearly be known
Until it has run its course and is considered to be grown

For each new child sown is great
Requiring the toiling of parents with an infinite faith
To bring forth the unique nature within the child's core
Means to nurture it, to praise it, and raise it to develop even more
And, if the child is given the right attention,
Would exceed expectations beyond what could be mentioned

To toil a seed — only the beginning of life's journey
But, to raise a seed — to have it reach a level of spiritual maturity - to produce good fruit just as the brances of a tree
A unique call to labor and a course to plot and earn life's lessons

Confirms the acts of nature's symbols of miracles
To toil of a seed — to witness its revelation of reflection as a definite testimony for the power within nature
The symbol in nature for the cycle of giving to receive the most honorable blessing

The Veins of the Earth

So does the earth have veins!
Its wealth runs through the valleys of its body and pours into its belly
Revolving and evolving…
Branching out to all nature's limbs

Its state is of many sizes and forms
Visible and invisible,
Wet and dry,
Feeds all of the earth's seed — as nature's laboring relies

To carry such a life force of substance and wealth
A grand symbol of being a true magistrate of so many states
What a hand to be dealt!

So, who is the laborer of this body carrying such a task to sustain life?
Providing all the earth's elements the necessary substances to live and to thrive!
The lifeline to all natures of the earth — the infinite reflections of miracles casted down from the sky
Valid enough reason to value all substances of life

The Carrier of Life

Soft, invisible and real…

I can feel its body wrap around mine…
Soothing me,
Letting me know that I'm alive

It's natural…
It's constant…
It's full of energy!

It stirs my attention in a direction
Steering with free navigation
Sharing the gifts of nature

It seems to always know where it's going
With a purpose, so well defined
Leaving reflective opportunities to recapture
The moment soon left behind

A wealthy giver…

The carrier of life!

It is very much alive, but has no visible heart, veins, or brain
And no matter — wherever it goes…
All of the earth's elements know it by name!

The symbol in nature for the universal breath and energy life force

A Cycle

A state of living in a state
For just a period of time…
Only to come out of it
To turn something around

To create some act of holistic motion
To evolve and yet, stay together
With each new revolving message
To bring about a change

For, if one cares to know…
The true messages — it deeds
Will deliver a state of constant growth
And a much purer seed

The generating of one's energy for life
To harvest a lesson learned
To repeat only one cycle while living upon the earth
To grow from each lesson earned

To make more clear "understanding"
With the movement of nature's symbol of time
A symbol in nature of a traveling shell guided by a core that is very much alive
The transition of coming into the light and out of the blind

The Harvest

No hollow shell can deliver a life
And no state of a cycle can take root and grow

If the seed sown has no core within it — no place to call "home"
Then nature cannot share the wealth and substance — to deliver her eternal hope

A home should offer a cycle of life's lessons
Yields the unity of the symbols — to live within and learn
Through the nurturing of the woman, as the He intended
Collecting the guidance and leadership of the man

Whatever is sown will be harvested…

Nature's Tears

For years…
Nature has been crying tears
A symbol of purification
To maintain its beauty by washing away impurities
A natural way of rejuvenation

So as the clouds capture the dust and hold it to delay,
Pressure builds from that which is captured and with-held from the sky
Until a time that it be cycled back into purification
Collected from the earth unsettled
And released through a cry

The dust symbolizes the residue that has been lost from its nest
Disturbed, held, and then released from the interacting of earth's elements
And has found no home to rest

For, when the clouds are dark
Is surely a symbol for the need to release…
Bringing about a brighter day and only after nature has shed its tears
A true symbol cycled to maintain infinite peace

To offer the dust another opportunity and a brand new life of worth
By bringing it forth among the living by settling it in the dirt

So do we cry for many a reason…
Symbolic of the change in living through each season

If we do not cry, we become dry and bitter spirits of crust
Like cracked mud that becomes broken and unsettled dust

With no ability to nurture life in an unsettled state so fragile
Bring back the beauty of nature's tears
To give new life to the core of the soul eternal
Simply to rejuvenate the spirit to live for many years

So, when the darkness follows the day, nature allows the time to release the strife
An offer to take a rest in the joys of living
And make solid the blessings of life

A new day will come again
It will offer an opportunity to live life's lessons learned
Providing a light to guide the way and an appreciation for all of our years
Simply by realizing the symbol of rejuvenation given through the purification of nature's tears

Nature's Symbol of Time

Like clockwork, the earth evolves on…
And every element in it changes its state of being
A process of purification, indeed…
With hope to join the Magistrate at home

The wisdom of the universe — the He that guides the way
to the knowledge that the earth possesses
Carries the nurturing force that life will stay

To feed a seed knowledge and to expect it to grow
Time can only be in wisdom — in each new seed as
they are sown

Nature's symbol of time
The evolving into a state of mind
To die in the flesh and to be born in the spirit
With each new mountain moved and climbed

Time has been given many names to represent its
forming,
But, it truly has a unique outfit which metamorphs with
growing

From weak to strong
From young to old
From least to many
From blind to wise
We are all blessed to know we've evolved and grown
through …

Nature's symbol of time

Chime, chime, chime…

From Dawn to Dusk

The moment there is dawn
The Waking Giant calls us
To meet the call to labor
Until, the end of dusk

The cycle of remembrance…
To meet that call again and again
To bear a fruit by the sweating of a brow
And to know the wages of all symbols in nature

The dawn brings the earth to sight
And the dusk brings her to darkness
A symbol of an empty shell
The need to be given light

Revealing the opposites of nature through the cycles of time
A cycle of symbols in nature to remember —
to feed our state until we are no longer blind

Nature's Symbol of a Back Breaker

It's small
And it's not lazy at all…
When nature calls
The job gets done!

Always on the move
To make a difference…

It endures all conditions
The whole year around
Making each call to labor
Building up from the ground

It has no clock but is always aligned with the time
It has no spine but a genius mind

It travels on a trail
A path with a direction
It searches with confidence
And a natural motivation

It never travels in a pair
But guarantees a partner is near
Each has its own mission in making a contribution
The true sign of equality and independent worth

Its strength is enormous
A heap raised above its head
Much more than its own weight — it claims its findings
To store in reserve so others are fed

It cares for its own
If by chance one falls…
A common gesture of respect
That's shared among all

Such a large and wise addition in nature's disposition
For such a small and overlooked position, and is definitely…

Nature's symbol of a back breaker

Pushed Away

A seed pushed away the crust...
And up from the mother earth
Raised a trunk so bold,
With its arms stretched toward the universe
And a reach so wide it appeared to celebrate its infinite existence
Embraced its freedom
Each arm covered in the armored shell of bark that symbolized its toughness in nature
For having claimed, nurtured, preserved and endured so many forms of life over the years
Bore the fruit of its own life through the seed from the arms and buds it bred
And in the heart of its bosom rested a nest
Surrounded by its arms and shaded by its leaves
Held the most free form of life on earth
The bird with wings must leave to catch its first flight to reach the sky
To gain confidence in the feathers which allow it to float on the soft carrier of life
Being held high above the earth to soar and still to labor to feed its seed
Requires an act of faith
It has to be pushed away

Man, raised up from the dirt of the earth
Stood boldly as a tree, but free to move about the earth as a bird
Spread and extended his arms toward the universe to

revive his soul
And claimed the very freedom that cannot be bought
or sold
A value of faith demonstrated by the view of nature's
rewarding symbols
Such is the symbol in nature to live from the buds that
blossom from its seed
When the bud was full, it pushed away its shell and
delicately spread its wings
Giving life to the leaf having veins
Pushed away from the very branch that gave to it a life
To cycle down to the dirt of the earth to bring forth new
birth
And gave life to so many forms of symbols through the
bearing of many fruit
A symbol of life so close to man
The veins that cycle life are the intertwine of all na-
ture's seed
Like the veins of the earth and the universe are reflect-
ed as the branches of a tree
What a level of growth that only evolves through time
and age
Even in all its might, it still sheds tears, as its sap is
released from its shell
To preserve its state — must sacrifice and labor its
way to live
By releasing the fruit with the ripened age reached
The same for all other symbols in nature…
Must be pushed away

The Supreme Beam

What a bulb!
Sends light down to the earth from the sky above
It sits so high and shines so bright
No inhabitant upon the earth can look upon it without going blind

Such a Symbolic Giant for all of nature's sake
Humbles all of nature
A necessity to view our path in life
The ultimate vein for all of nature
And, demands its very state

The Supreme Beam
What a sight!

Its rays are ever present someplace upon the earth
Stretching out many arms to embrace the universe
Giving all of nature the opportunity to appreciate its universal worth

Such a Symbolic Giant to all of nature's seed
A necessity for growing humbleness - planting the desire to be freed

The Supreme Beam
What a feeling!

And when it sets at the end of a day
Allows the coolness to come and transforms the beauty of its colored reflections
Reigns upon the earth's horizon
To create a visual masterpiece — on a canvas so widely adorned
It kisses both the earth and the sky
Such a Symbolic Giant to all of nature's view
Even with such a high position — a part of the rainbow too!

The Supreme Beam
What beauty!

The element of the beam is so all powerful and pure
It generates the energy for the symbols in nature to carry life and endure

Such a Symbolic Giant to all of nature's nurturing
Offers the joys of light, humbleness, beauty and living

The Supreme Beam
What majesty!

The Queen of Night

The calming beam of light
Makes her appearance to the mother earth at night
To cool her garment and to give to her rest
Yet, to give to her some sight, at best…

The queen's eloquently glazed surface
Allows the universe to look upon her face
A cycle of being humble to the Waking Giant
A symbol of her nature and His grace

Her beauty is the brightest among the night's stars
She sits high in her large seat to please
And to remind all elements of the earth
To kneel down - and men to their knees

To cycle the symbol in nature — a reflection
Among all the universe
To purify the affection of nurturing
Down to the mother earth

The Queen of Night
The symbol in nature that offers rest and thankfulness,
reminding us all to receive the opportunity given to get
life right

The Genders of Nature

As with everything else, nature shares a relationship of he and she
The very nature that allows the earth to evolve and to create life
It is most common for the symbols of nature to take on a gender
To define their role by developing chores to tender

These states of position are true to God's purpose
To generate pure seed and to set them free
Making man in His own image and the woman from man's rib
The possibility to reassign a position within this state
And to imply their condition be...
Can only be an act of a weed chasing a seed...

If a tree grows to the level of maturity and has the ability to bear fruit from its seed
Then the ultimate chore of maintaining its position
to multiply is pretty much concrete...

The sun is the light that he bears the world with sight
And the moon is the pillow that he lays his head at night
Then the stars are the children that nature has multiplied
To create a family, oh so beautiful and to keep this earth alive
For the universal nature of the earth — referred to as a she
Holds the powerfful channels carrying the nurturing substances within her belly to yield the shell of seed
Although this reference of nurturing power is given to her — to bear
Can only deliver a fruit when combined with the energy

of its opposite power — to pair
Therefore, the nurturing power of the she depends on the transforming power of the he
When combined, creates the ultimate power of labor to deliver good ripened fruit, pushed away from the shell of the she, the seed, as from the branches of a tree

And any time the nature of the earth is given to the he
Goes far beyond the shell to yield its life, the core, enveloped by the universe to breed its true nature — eternally
References the guidance for the core within the shell of all earth's seed
Must live within the state of unions to be forever binded by the laws of the universe — life's eternal deed
The genders of nature establish life's balance for all energy forms to recreate
Equalizes the labor life requires, toils from the trunk of opposite genders — to mate

The combination of the he and the she, manifests the true power of a union to deliver reflections — nature's universal miracle
Extended branches of life, the veins bearing beautiful fruit with fertile seeds embedded within each core — states Innocent and PURE and oh, so plentiful

The positions of he and she will stand within the state of their union forever
This call to labor life's beautiful garden requires of both the chore of tendering together
The symbols in nature for replenishing of the earth with good seed

Why Opposites Attract

What is the equivalent of the opposite?
Why ask why?
Why opposites attract…

Are opposites less valuable?
If so…
What elements do they lack?

The equator is an imaginary line that circles and separates the surface of the earth into opposite halves
Still, the energy of the universe holds them together
And somehow pulls them back!
To delliver equally - the distribution of earth's opposite two states in the making of its whole

The two parts stand in opposite positions to define and carry out nature's ultimate chore
Together, they offer one big revelation for the earth's true natures - opens life's two substantial doors
North and south are the symbols that divide all life among the states of cold and hot
For they both are entrances held open and leads into the two natures possessed within nature's core
Branches out their opposites from any direction or position on the earth's surface and allows the free will for man to choose which door to enter
To always yield our attention back to the center of its cracked and tarnished shell, to reveal, divide and clearly define the core nature of our souls
Transforms our very state of life through the nurturing of choice, time and age to be one or the other
To become enlightened in the ways of self and in the ways of another

A positive and a negative are opposite and yet, they attract hand to hand
And similarly, the opposition is set forth upon this earth and is yet, the test of man

In order for man to understand the chores of life and to complete each task assigned...
He must evolve by carrying both natures of life's state to reach purity — given the mind that develops a spine
Challenged to bring forth understanding and to keep man on a true search to find
The value in the differences — one to the other
To bring forth wisdom to man - his delivery out of the blind
The only way of providing guidance
To keep man traveling — in line
To have him balance his own struggle in life through learning the "POWER OF CHOICE!"
To gain the fortitude by which to make a decision
To make clear, from any direction, the position of his stand - a reflection

Just know — the universe will always lead the way
A negative magnifies and exalts the positive by comparison of their states among all of creation

The symbols in nature that establishes the scale of appreciation

To Be Pure

Stage by stage…
The transformation of age!
The process of toiling the natural mineral of the earth with each given day
Brings about the quality of a pure state,
But only after it has been processed to withstand the test
For the laboring, alongside and with the law of the land
As each stage is carefully fermented and guided by the Magistrate's Hand

To be pure…
Determined by its creator
And the substance therein will not be graded — until it has matched its successor's gauge
Whatever is created — will reflect the natures of its creator
And to master the state of purity — runs parallel to its equator
The purity of a state gives equal values to all its positions just the same
So simply, reflection justifies the sure calling of your name - rest assured, your journey is not in vain…
Because you would never have been created and not be offered the same

To be pure…
Running the course of this life to endure
Knowing that you will be graded
Only when you have met the passing score

Stage by stage
The transformation of age
To be pure…
An acquired state
Acceptance of the cleansing grace from the Magistrate

Dust of the Earth

Do the dirt and the dust of the earth forever cling?
They each have a hand in everything

Somehow, the cycle of rejuvenation
Keeps these two in line with eternal life - earth's revelation

The state at the beginning and the state of the end
Will always include the dirt and the dust of the dear, mother earth

So, the transformation of all of earth's elements
Are here only for a while and are most energetic

First given a form that is full of mass - and in time, evolves into an energy that is most angelic

The dust is released from the dirt and then taken away from the mother earth
Symbolizing the process for removing impurities and the need to be cleansed

It's taken to the highest level toward the universe, to the clouds that fill the sky
To be purified, rejuvenated, and to returned to the earth through a cry

To join up with the dirt again
Upon the mother earth survived
Impacted with the right ingredients
To keep this earth alive

Crystal of the Earth

A natural cure
So delicate and light
It floats down to the earth
To unify the symbols of nature's might
For it is the only element of the earth that embraces them all
To give them the same visible face
By bringing them to attention to answer its call
A symbol in nature to cycle — only one pure state
The most pure and versatile state of nature
With its cool color and state so pure
It compliments the rays of the sun
And settles on the earth
A warm welcome for the crystal of the earth

The ironic reality about this symbol in nature
It coats and covers the earth just like a jacket
Yet, it cools and calms the earth to settle all its movement
Just to bring forth the pleasures of laboring seed
Giving life back upon its leaving

Such a valuable symbol in nature
When its job is done will also kneel completely to the sun
To melt away and to offer the earth its nutrients
By quenching the thirst of all that were so faithful to be found at home
To receive the gift of life through the toast of a drink,
And all together…
With the crystal of the earth

Reflections

We're all the same
No matter what the name
The truest miracle that we will ever behold
To see the universal reflections in each element known
The elements of the dirt and dust

The water that brings them back to earth
The veins of the earth that carry life through its belly
To feed all of the earth's elements
The journey through each transformation
The carrier of life through pollination
A cycle of a symbol for the revelation
The reflections of life are all around us
The transfering of directions for man to follow

As each element depends on another
To survive and thrive, one seed must consume the other
So, the shell acts as an armor to protect and preserve its very state
To provide the earth elements with the food to rejuvenate
A cycle of symbols in nature that transforms life through a vein to all of earth's creations

Even the very seed that is sown into the soil does have a shell of armor
The wearing of a shell around the core to protect it and to nurture it to show its face
And, if it is hollow, will not yield to the state of nurturing reflections that the laboring for life eternal requires
A sure symbol of reflections we will find in the mother earth - the knowing that a shell is present, does not always reflect a living core

This proves that the laboring of a seed beneath its shell is required for its life evermore

Flesh and Bones

To understand this barren land, the shell of flesh and bones...Created by the He to preserve the frailty of the earth; the core of nature's soul, laid before Him, the states of innocent beauty and pure worth. So man was, at the beginning of time, the only two symbols adorned by the vein that delivered the innocence and purity of all earth's symbols. The wealth of nature's soul was placed in the garden to live eternally, until the shell was tarnished after mixing with the darkened lust of earth's temptations and the states were taken away

And man became a tarnished shell with a lost core to find, in a state of the shell being in the dark, naked and blind. Now, only born to meet the call to labor, man's flesh and bones, must now travel through life's cycle of purification to earn back the original worth and to save the pureness of his soul - by toiling and laboring in the natural raw earth from which he was made, to divide the two natures again - now so intertwined within his core, stained and emptied, the vein of eternal life

Each man must reestablish a vein to nurture the plant of likeness by sowing the seeds of His Light to bridge with His Spirit. Given after the fall into darkness, to pit the darkened thorns of lust from within his fragile core by choosing between the earth's two substantial doors (natures), to extend and rejuvenate his own vein of life, to be refilled, purified and delivered eternally. The shell of flesh and bones will be put back into the raw state of the dirt and dust of earth's floor to be recycled

The purification and rejuvenation of Flesh and Bones
Away from the state of darkness and the hollow kind,
A shell of light delivered and sown
For the dark, hollow, naked and blind

Journey of a Lifetime

You will never take another trip so grand
Than to travel through the cycle of symbols in nature

Tasting the joys of the fruit it does bear
Savoring the life of a seed that's spared

Knowing your state within the symbol each holds
By following nature's guidance while measuring the weight of your soul

To have witnessed each state, therein...
To realize the values in laboring above darkness

To bring into clear focus the Supreme Beam of truth, indeed
To gain a state when the flesh and bones are no longer of need and the soul is set free

To find that you have reached the state to endure
To have traveled the journey across the mother earth to a state that's pure

A cycle of travel through this life required of all symbols in nature

Innocent and PURE...

To Be Transformed

To be or not…
        Willing
To show or not…
        Thankfulness
To accept or not…
        His one precious gift
To show or not…
        Commitment
To labor or not…
        Upon the mother earth
To show or not…
        Faithful service
To nurture or not…
        The core of a seed
To show or not…
        Acts of love and giving life
To be transformed or not…
        From the flesh into the spirit
To show or not…
        Faith
To be free or not…
        The core of the soul
To show or not…
        Worth
To live or not…
        Eternally

Nature's Scale

Measures the weight of a state with age,
When it is pressed against the temperature gauge,
Will determine where the register stands
To identify the need at hand

The cycle of symbols for measurement
Giving direction to the earth's elements
Keeping them all aligned
With nature's symbols of time

Temperature Gauge

Cold or hot…
Hot or cold…
The temperature gauge
Measures the soul

It measures by day and by night
Against all of the symbols of the mother earth
And to keep us living right

For the Supreme Beam is a cycle of warmth
And the Queen of Night the cycle of cool
Working together, both dawn and dusk
The gracious symbols reflecting the eternal rule

The reading will be either — hot or cold
Not in between…

Spine

Why have a spine?

A spine keeps us in line
It keeps the body straight
It signals to the body when its makeup is going astray
And, if it falls out of sorts
It gives us such a pain

The cycle of the spine that labors
A bite from a small element delivering a powerful waiver
A signal to remember…
Nature's symbol of a back breaker

The Evolution of Motion

Is it a cycle or a destination?

The movement of a form or energy
Evolving into a newness
To bring about a change

It's pure freedom...

Is it a symbol or a system?

The status of a state
The way to navigate
On the course of purpose — a direction

It's life...

Is it a vein?

Visible or invisible
An amazing reality
The way to measure growth

The evolution of motion is a necessity that carries transformations and states of progress!

A Song of Harmony

Bring back the joys of the sounds
Joys make for harmony beneath the clouds

Listen to nature…
Oh hear an orchestra with its superb unity
Celebrating the life of living in the beauty of earth's garden
With free access to all its fruit
No need for pardon…
There's plenty to go around

Hear the sounds
A song of harmony

For the symbols of the earth are in one accord
And the rhythm of the motion in line with its heartbeat

Rejoice in its purity
A crystal clear and eclectic tone
The feeding of spirits until they have grown
To sing out loud and to be heard among the clouds
With free will to access the fruit of life
No need for pardon…
There's plenty to go around

Hear the sounds
A song of harmony

Listen to the messages as they soothe the soul
The lyrics are known and sung by each creature young and old

Such a beautiful sound
Reigning throughout the universe
The majestic chimes of a celebration
For freedom is the universal song for each of God's nations
No need for pardon…
There's plenty to go around

Join in and sing a song of harmony

Universe

It's all around us
The creation of the He that sets us free

For if there was no universe we would have no place to gaze
To imagine what comes after this earth
We could never be amazed

It's a very wondrous sight to bring into view
To behold its very elements is to magnify its might
No matter what time we may find to give to it
By day or by night

It carries all of the glorious elements, you see...
The Sun, the Moon, the Stars and Earth
Allowing us just a little taste of purity
From the land of milk and honey

Magnificently arranged and so perfectly aligned
The interacting of its makeup
Keeps us looking up…
Keeps us counting the time

The vision of reaching that marvelous city
Some place beyond the sky
To walk the streets that are paved with gold
Delivers the symbols in all of nature to define the core of its soul…

To be rich with the elements
From the veins that nurture the mother earth
Learning from each of her cycled symbols
And sharing in her giving birth

To learn to live among its glorious elements
We trust they are here to stay
But the true growth lesson of life — to know
We will all leave some day

To be freed from all our labors rendered
To count the seed that we have tendered
Together...
We will all continue to live forever

Such a gracious gesture of nature
To share in the joys of life upon this earth
Guiding us through our climb
Until our labor has met its worth

The universal compass...

The Rainbow Effect

How miraculous is this symbol?

It generates the variety of life
Two by two
It's where it all began…
The rainbow effect is our reminder and opportunity to conquer this life again

The he and the she
To make a pair, a colorful reflection revealed
To coil, toil, and labor to deliver the energy of nature's will
The combining of the formulas for creating the spirit of good fruit…
A reflection of the tree that bred them
Reflecting the image and the color of truth

The reminder of our hope for a long life upon this earth and the opportunity to sow our seed
The joyous symbol of colorful living while on this earth and beyond the rainbow indeed…

The rainbow effect is full of vibrant colors and spreads life's seed across the sky
More often than not, will come to greet us after nature has taken a cry
A rejoicing symbol for shedding tears of joy while laboring to become pure
To have birthed a seed that created a vessel willing to carry the substances possessed for life to endure
With each new seed offers a vein to the core of Mother Nature
By performing the very same act of labor that was performed at the birth of creation

For the clay of the earth and man are of many colors
And each has its place in the joys of its mother

The rainbow effect is our reminder to appreciate the joys of the differences around
To know that each is required to build the bridge that travels the route, eternal bound

Two by two
The true vessels of substance build the bridge that leads to the crystal city so grand…
The many vessels of wiser men spread across the earth holding hands
So do we cry upon the earth…
While blending our valuable differences with each new birth
Reflections of crystals, a falling star to catch
To toil and labor, to mend and prepare the colorful garments
To be worn when the time comes to receive a crown to match

The rainbow effect will be the roll book used when God calls the names of men
To weigh the values of the seed produced and to deliver them away from sin

The rainbow effect reflects the hands that miraculously toiled the earth's natures to deliver the soul of every color of man

The cycle of a symbol in nature that should bring to our remembrance the hope for life evermore

The Core of a Seed

Have you ever wondered about the state within the core of a seed?

It lives in a shell possessing the most fertile spot
The shell is hard and yet, the core is not
Because the core is the place where nature placed the heart
It carries the force of life and lives in the most central part
And, to taste of it, delivers the sweetest flavor
For all good fruit found in Mother Nature

A cycle of a symbol in nature that gives richness and wealth to the fruit of life

The Fertile Seed

It is more than an empty shell…
It has a core

It is the core that gives to it life…
It breathes

Its life comes out of the dark and stands in the light…
It is seen

The fertile seed can breed…
It gives new life

It carries the light…
To feed the hollow seed

To meet the call to labor…
To earn eternal life

It is free…

The Hollow Seed

It is nothing more than a shell…
It is empty

There is not a core to hold life…
It cannot breathe

It sits in the dark…
It is lost

A hollow seed cannot breed…
It is dead

It is in need of the light…
It must be fed

From the toils and labors of a fertile seed…
So life will be given

It can be freed…

Mind

The head of all the body…

Collects, composes and filters the messages of nature's voice and distributes substances for maintaining life within its core
And, if it is starved — will yield no direction
No means of reflection
No home to plant or toil a seed

A laborer of many deeds — lined into rows
The creation of a garden
Nurtured with the wealth of understanding
The ways for successful navigating

The watch that keeps time, as it grows wiser…

The bearing of more good fruit to shine…

A cycle of a symbol in nature for purpose and leadership

Heart

The core cadence of the universe…

Carrying the rhythm of the beat
Reciprocating nature's will to feed
All limbs extended from its shell
As the song of harmony is sung
Throughout eternity will always tell

It is the vessel that sings out loud
The condition of its core and the state of its mind

A cycle of a symbol in nature that receives and gives
life from a vein carrying substances of wealth

Spirit

It's there…
Remember?

The conscious guiding with might
The intertwining of the He within nature to deliver to all,
His Light

Delivering the cycle of symbols into nature's ear
Our vessel for hearing the call when "They" are near

Soul

Everyone knows…
There is a soul to be reckoned with!

The matter of its condition
To carry its petition
To believe or not…

So, surely the choice is made
To state from where it stands
With either the He — the creator of its relief
Or, to settle to the darkened ways of lowly man

No need to argue this revelation
Just realize the cycle of symbols in nature
To be transformed…

For the time will surely come again
When the Waking Giant shall call the soul
To make known the seed it has sown

The Gift of Giving

The most honorable symbol of the universe
Passing on the symbols and substances of wealth

Its cycle is the product of a good seed

To Receive

The acknowledgment of a need
Accepting the symbols and substances of wealth

Its cycle is the product of receiving good seed

To Quench Your Thirst

To drink of the substance that was offered up for you
From the He who gave His Light just to give you truth

A most precious sacrifice to create a vein from Him to you
A vessel that is filled with the worth of His varied positions and states

Nurtures all the seed carrying the core that is receptive to the abundance of veins streaming from the symbols offered through the messages of nature's voice saying, "DRINK the state of overflowing wealth from the fruit generated from His Light"

To quench your thirst and to rectify your state
To live beyond the state of the flesh to receive the purification of your spirit from His saving grace

A symbol in nature for purification of your vessel as you travel across the bridge…

To Feed Your Hunger

To eat the fruit borne of the mother earth and seeded by the universe
To take up the Light in your shell to labor

To walk in line with those who travel toward the sowing of good seed within the mind
Tasting the fruit of truth and the meat of His Word
— while traveling toward the land of milk and honey
Transferred through the symbols in nature that feed the spiritual core within the body it binds

To receive the call to labor, to bear a fruit that's ripe
By toiling the spiritual core within your physical shell
With the plants of eternal life

A symbol in nature for rejuvenation of your vessel as you travel across the bridge...

To Rest

To lean upon the Light that gives the earth its sight
To realize that our purpose is to wield His very might

To know that no other energy can carry a weight so heavy
With hands to deliver life's substances to all, in plenty
Unifies the need of all nature's cycle of symbols,
The gift of eternal relief

Resting assured the day to come…
To rid the shell that carried the seed of Light upon this earth
The shell of flesh and bones no longer needed
Will be put back to earth and the soul will be greeted

After the time that nature gave to each to purify its core
Yields a measurement of the worth for the labors it bore

To rest is to know where you stand…

To Move a Mountain

The peak time to meet the call to labor
When up against the challenge to stay in line…
The need to keep in mind
The need of the spine

The spine aligns the mind, heart, body, spirit and soul
Allows the strength to cycle forward and through the times when life is cold
To carry the light in the time of darkness - be BOLD!
To move the steepest and heaviest of labors…
Just knowing that the core of its nature is also…

Innocent and PURE…

The Beauty of a Garden

Imagine, a garden that is filled
With the most precious fruit in all the mother earth
And each of them has made the call to labor
No longer hollow, but fertile seed and able

So diligently working from dawn to dusk
No fruit is in the dark, but carries a light with trust
Each delivers life to the cycle of a good seed
For they are inspired by the nature of the symbols, indeed

To share of its cycles to keep them all Innocent and PURE
As they are all aligned with the nature of the times
Their veins carry the wealth from the vessels of the He
The He who made the purest sacrifice, to set them free

They are universal in their song of harmony that chimes
Each wears the shell of flesh and of bones and has within it a spine
Determined to carry the light that will lead them home
Traveling faithfully across the bridge from here to there, but not alone

And enjoying its gifts along the way
Quenching their thirst and feeding their hunger both night and day
Realizing that each fruit must labor in order to receive
While taking the time to rest by dropping down to their knees

And humbly bowing under the queen of relief at the nightfall
Collecting their state and preparing to answer with the

Waking Giant's call
Acknowledging the presence of the Supreme Beam
Carrying the significant symbols of faith and a back-breaking team

Each stands up against the temperature gauge
Stepping on the scale of nature each cycle of the way
Their evolution of motion from the flesh to the spirit
Has transformed them all and set them free for deliverance

Reflecting on the transformations and the wisdom given
To value the core from the harvest that is deeply rooted
The rainbow of a commitment to be a carrier of life
Moving mountains in the time of darkness and strife

A cycle of symbols in nature that we are all in need
Each wearing a different shell but carrying a worthy seed
To wear the crown of life, when at the end, each will be fitted

And the labors upon the earth have, no doubt, been completed
The crystal of the earth will toast, "Undefeated!"

Each being pushed away to bring home its own faith
They faithfully shed nature's tears to purify their state
Traveling through this garden is definitely the journey of a lifetime
With all singing a song of harmony....
We are no longer in the dark, hollow, naked and blind!

The Crown of Life

The majestic existence of the earth
Does wear a crown…
And its crests sparkle among all symbols around

It is the most privileged symbol in all of nature
As it stands tall and bold above all of creation
Reaching high toward the universe

It is truly the most powerful symbol of nature
And, is challenged all year around
Its might is simply its position of calm, stacked up from the ground

All of earth's creatures want a taste of it
Man, to say the least…
To challenge its strength just for the sake of it
To simply reach its peak
To experience its serenity and infinite peace
And no matter what the cost — does labor to conquer its possessions
The ultimate level of challenging raw earth — to wave the hand of a legend

It is enormous in size
Yet, sits so still among the skies

It offers a place of tranquility despite all its might
Standing high above the earth by day
Still reverenced by the night

It, no doubt, already wears the crown of life
Standing tall and bold when challenged…
Still, yet the most humble

Hard Pillars

The burdens held by nature's will to survive lays on the hard pillars of day-to-day living
Resting on the crests of all her columns of labor
Carrying the load of specific chores as each was given
Delivering one harvest of wealth in substances to bear all — good favor

Mended together, the columns build the bridge from here to there
Across all of nature's transitions to travel the distance fair
Shares the load of establishing one existence of an equally weighted state
Balance above and through each season of life to thrive and preserve faith

Plants many seeds of unique growth to reflect a beautiful garden having one core
For all to cycle the purification and rejuvenation to reach and enter life's eternal door
Stands the position of strength for all to reveal one direction toward a unified might
Signals the way to cross from the barren land through and by the vein of nature's reflection of eternal light

The symbol in nature that reveals the power in understanding unity and the way to lighten the burdens of the load carried from here to there

Lasting Impressions...

I can recall...

I can recall from childhood, watching the rain through
my bedroom window as it drizzled down from a place
unseen

I can recall hearing the sounds of the water as it
danced like pearls on the rooftop and rolled off the
edges to rest with such poise and discipline, like a
draped curtain stretched across my view to create a
small trench pressing into the earth

I can recall the distortion of the back yard — the place
where I played basketball
I focused on the many small puddles that formed
between the worn grassy areas that bared the sand,
states of barren land

I can recall a sound like a courageous lion roaring, and
sparks of majesty complimented its call by lighting up
the sky to guide its way

Reflections and shadows jumped to attention and the
darkness suddenly appeared again

The mystery and wonder of what was prowling in the
darkness beyond the edges of the yard kept my
unbroken attention

I pulled the covers over my head, leaving only a small
opening to keep my view

Time passed...
I can recall waking up to a bright sunny day!

Explanation Territory

Explanation…territory…
Whoever told the whole story?

Men walk upon the earth for only a moment...
Each allowed an opportunity to taste the joys of living
And the territory of earth he possesses during his time
Should be intertwined with all natures of giving

Who knows the exact time each man will stay?
Who truly has the power over his state?

And, who could possibly be the sole owner of earth's great state and territories?

Man's sole claims of earth's territories are only sorts of distractions, breaking up the wholeness of its wisdoms, as God planned; a wealthy number, down to fractions. The division of wealth in substances to be collected, tallied and taught to men across the globe. The only way to feed the knowledge of the earth and its nature to a man, so that He may feed man's soul. So, to feed one part of earth's territory and not consider its state in whole leaves an enormous hole in the state of man's mind and the core of his nature's soul.

The whole of earth is truly one big state, filled with " God's Family," the uniquely assembled colors of fruit delivering varieties of taste. The state of a family binds a man, woman and child, independently defining their uniquely arranged branches of territories, and yet its whole binds with the branches of other states. The states of men are so intertwined. Therefore, only one unique assembly of fruit will seek God's Light to bind

His Family, to taste the wholeness of life. No other mold can offer the original taste of God's Fruits and Glory, " the symbol of unity assembles and defines the wholeness of God's story," regardless of man's present existence in earth's state of territories. Ask yourself, are you really understanding "the WHOLE story?"

Again, there is no substitute for the true taste of God's original fruits; no other legitimate claim, because the world of light is one big state of territories where all men are branched out to eat and live, just the same. How does man claim to be so spiritually universal and still, be willing to ignore the fallen parts of nature's most fragile states? What vein of man travels through life consuming less fruit than collected and yet, ignores the needs of the poor?

If the whole of man survives the labors of living upon this earth and reaches a level of spiritual maturity, he will care to "yield a spiritual harvest grown" to be honored by God's kingdom, to be called His Family; truly offering everyone a place called "HOME." Yet, if any part of the whole is taken away before the process of man's delivery is complete, will starve all men, God's Children, to defeat spiritual growth. Therefore, all men continue to grope along in darkness. There will be no disassembly of the Body of Light, the tree that breeds the only fruit of eternal life. The only legitimate claim for living within God's cycle of unified symbols in nature. All other claims, they will not eat...

Explanation…territory…
I thought that I should tell the whole story!

Butterfly

The most beautiful creation of motion in all of nature
A tender reflection of a living rainbow to nurture
Possessing the purest blend of colors in spirit
Carries the freedoms apart from strife to explore new territories
Holding a position, having the lightest heart — free from worry
The state found within the core of a child — laboring freely to share the fruit of its journey

A symbol for the gentle nature of both states — innocence and purity, and the evolutions of freedoms they will forever hold and deliver

Deeply Rooted

The reality of the world awaits us all

Praised or dazed…
The ways that we are raised
Guided, or put into a maze

Don't be amazed
It's deeply rooted!

A weed doesn't require a seed to replenish itself
But a wild root tightly woven and naturally driven
To travel aggressively deep beneath the surface
Challenges the course of nature to generate a seed

The very seed that gives a seed
Is most always chased by a weed

So we as the seed of the earth
Must constantly labor to nurture a seed
From the chastening of the weed

Praised or dazed…
The ways that we are raised
Guided, or put into a maze

Make no mistake
It's deeply rooted!

Deny Me Not…

Deny me not my place in time
A harvest to yield a settled mind

Speaking words that are seldom heard
An echoing voice in a forest stirred

Free, but wanting to free another
The opportunity to break the barriers of this life together

Deny me not my quest to soar
Above this forest to understand more

And fly beyond the edges of what can be seen
Grasping the opportunity to generate more good seed

So, let us all sing a song to celebrate
The natural exploration of a newly found state

Eclipse

The event of the year…

The universe will witness the dance between the
Supreme Beam and the Queen of Night in celebration
of her eloquence and His magnificent might

A celebration that will seldom be missed
The great moment of time when the great elements will
kiss

An event that all the earth will call into view
To witness this glorious dance between the sun and
the moon

What a lovely stage, presented and decorated with
stars of crystal…
Gleaming and glittering among them all to signal
To announce the queen as she enters the door
They all bow down to give her the floor

The queen takes the floor to dance all around
Very center the sun and earth to spread her gown

Her gown is spread like a vibrant light, so soft and delicate
To make known her umbra before the sun to celebrate

So synchronized and skillful are the moon and the sun
As they line up in unison with the earth, one by one
To share in this dance, a universal celebration
Just a few moments when the sun, moon and earth are in equilibrium

The Supreme Beam gives this honor to the Queen of Night
This very special dance to share with Him, His might
For her to cast her shadow down below

No better view for the earth than a seat in the front row

A symbol in nature for alignment, balance and unity

The Colors of Wealth

The carpet of the earth is genius green

So close to the color of blue that can be seen
Rolled out for the world such wealth in meaning

From the farthest distance to reflect infinity
A symbol of wealth for life and eternity
Just as the sky yields to the color of blue
The blood that runs through the veins of man does, too

These colors are worn by all living elements
The grass, the trees and their leaves — among few

To the peaks of the mountains brought into view
Wears more boldly from a distance, the blend of the two
Even the ocean and the sea in their mass hold true
Reflect the colors of wealth,
Both green and blue

The Softness of a Rose Petal

The softness of a rose petal
The most precious of all…
Carries the sweet smell of Mother Nature
And a beauty so widely adorned

Its beauty is so natural and so pure when grown
Standing high on the throne
Yet, guarded by thorns

A symbol to identify the state of innocence is there
To lift it up with delicate care

The softness of a rose petal
A unique symbol in nature's design
Carries both the joys and pain of life
Extended from a vine

A vine that represents the lifeline as a vein
It carries the labors of a seed just the same

The symbol in nature for the softness of a rose petal
Brings to light the true state of beauty
And, the price for living…

On that Day

On that day…
Know your state

On that day…
Celebrate

On that day…
You'll be free

Eternally

Overflowing

Who is coming to dinner?
To share in the feast of truth…

Who has an invitation?
To enter this glorious celebration…

Who will bring a guest?
To be seated at the table with them abreast…

Who will set the table?
Place the plates, glasses, and utensils…

Who will fill the plates?
With the food of eternal life…

Who will pour the drinks?
Overflowing

Petrified

Sitting idle for too long and without life
Transforms nature's very state for being so still…
Taking on a state of stone — to the bone
To breathe no more
The hardening of its core
The shell worn will eventually reveal

A symbol in nature that says to us to move through life without allowing hardships to harden the core of our heart

Discretion

Travel with truth
The narrow lane
Life's most challenging course
Living the lessons learned
A true education earned
Destination bound…
Composed expectations
Symbolist of sight
Speak with substance
Oh, nature of direction…
A voice
Wave her messages sound…
Four seasons of time
A light is reflected…
Weighs in spectrum — the gown
Adorn to stand and shine — the crystal crown

Discretion

A cycle of symbols in nature for utilizing its wisdom while maneuvering through life

Expectations

Man's ultimate driving force
Defines the ways he views himself
And positions him within nature

It's the grid by which he plots his growth
And controls the lessons learned, at most...

The expectation to survive and thrive
To understand how to live among men
To travel through all of the rotations of living
To rid the grasps of sin

A symbol in nature that expresses the need for sight
By establishing a definite direction toward a destination
To keep man looking up and reaching high

What are your life expectations?

Nature

An existence of energy...

The natural makeup of a composition
Influenced by its state or position
Evolving into or out of a condition
The adaptation to free will and the need to survive

Acts of Nature

You…

Be…

The judge...

The way you choose
The way you perceive
The way you think
The way you love
The way you believe
The way you respond
The way you adapt
The way you treat yourself
The way you feel
The way you travel
The way you sow
The way you give
The way you treat others
The way you serve
The way you learn
The way you grow
The way you know
The way you labor
The way you receive
The way you appreciate
The way you transform
The way you live
The way you succeed
The way you survive
The way you thrive

These are your acts of nature…

Sensitive by Nature

To feel
To laugh
To cry
To question…
Why?

To hope
To dream
To try
To change…
A state of mind

To think
To know
To grow
To believe…
In the word "I"

To be sensitive by nature
Hearing each message in nature's voice
Echoing throughout her universal makeup
And the positions of her very individual states

To care to "Identify"
With each part of a being
Comes first by understanding the makeup of one's
own position
The very state of being sensitive by nature
To almost everything

To find the value in the state of each "Individual"
To see each makeup in parts and in whole
By realizing the lessons that each can teach

When searching the core of each soul

To know the relevance of each nature to “Inspire”
Through the free sharing of experiences from each position held
As each is generated by nature’s state and is issued to them accordingly
To carry an individual with a unique message, to spread one to the other

To be sensitive by nature
A simple makeup that each has in common
To assist and to maintain the states of being Innocent and PURE
As each was placed upon this earth from the very beginning

To feel that each is valued by all others around
To laugh with each individual to recall that sound
To cry when one has lost the way of standing firm
To question why each does cry, delivers solutions for each to understand and learn

To hope that each does well in the state where each stands
To labor for each individual’s succeeding beyond the barren sand
To pass on the wisdom and hopeful thoughts

To change a state of mind as each wise man sought

To think and see beyond that which is obvious to the eye
To know more by mapping the travel and keeping the coins close in hand
To grow while plotting and paving the way for others, to guide them across that very land
To believe in the words that each must conquer, very simply, the words, "I can"

To be sensitive by nature
To show "Interest" in each individual voice
The echoes of the states and positions of a makeup
The need to receive symbols of encouragement given freely, one to another

Why does nature reflect such individual states and positions that are so intertwined?

It's the universal symbol of nature's voice that delivers us all a hand to assist in the deliverance of man from the state of being in the dark, naked and blind

A demonstrated model and compass toward such a valuable message…

"Look closer, look deeper…"

Crusty Mud

Always after the rain…
The dirt and the dust
Will bond together and dry
To become a crusty mud

Its state is very unsettled
For it had to take a cry
To get through the storm that challenged it
Hope descended from the sky

To step on the state of crusty mud
While in a fragile state so fine
Will surely break its spine and efforts to labor
The hope to stay in line

The act of nature to recreate life
Must be delivered from the burdens of its strife
By transforming its composition back into the earth's veins
To a state capable of bearing fruit, and the position to regain its might

The Mineral of the Earth

Iron or steel
Copper or brass
Diamonds or pearls
Silver or gold

The list goes on and on…

Each was transformed
To reach its purest form

Isn't it amazing?
The mineral of the earth that we're craving…
The most expensive sold!

The mineral of the earth is free
But the transformation process requires labor
By an order to have it transduced
Initiated by the sole producer
And the one who reaps the fruit

Isn't it grand?
When applying this concept of transformation to the soul of man…

The richest elements within the mineral of man have already been paid!

The symbols in nature's voice that reflect the laboring approach required of man to reach from here to there

The Element of Energy

The element of energy moves mountains
The very invisible energy that moves nature forward
The cycling of symbols that carries the hidden messages
Offered to collect and create a composition of truth within the mind of man
The exertion to have him learn from experiences and to make substance of the finds
The element of energy is a constant reality of nature's fate and is certainly of many kinds

The element of energy may be one of either good or bad
Exercised through the very act of making a choice, a reality sown
The coiling and creating of a seed to labor, and to live through each spirit known
Collected, composed and distributed to the surroundings by each laboring hand

To pass, to linger for a while, or to stay forever
The element of energy is a collaborative force that impresses the nature of all life endeavors

The element of energy changes a state or position
The very natural inclination to maintain, at the least, or to reach a more unique existence
Gives birth to each lesson captured, learned and applied while living through transitions
The major influence in the makeup of nature's core composition
Endorsed and presented by the universal nature of man's will to survive and stand
To bring forth the better makeup of the self and the true spirit of the land

A symbol in nature that depicts man's influences on evolution

To Walk on Water

Literally, an amazing feat to perform…
Only One has in the flesh…

But all can in the spirit…
By composing and exercising a higher level of faith
To walk across the most sensitive nature of life's situations
To rise above it and to pass it
Without being disturbed, engulfed or consumed

To meet the challenge of crossing over from here to there
Requires one to see and to hear
The messages within nature's transitional seasons
Hurled at man repeatedly for these many reasons
And during the most trying of times…

To walk on water

Requires a belief…
To act in the spirit of calm…
The reinforced cycle of thought during travel

The symbol in nature that offers a pass to get through the roughest of storms

The Children of the Garden

They are the seed of the earth…

Planted deeply into the core of nature's will
To generate the state of innocence over and over again
And reigns the richness of living from the substance therein…

The land of milk and honey

Their voices echo throughout the universe singing the song of harmony
Carrying the state of the fruit from the tree which bred them
Walking, running, jumping and dancing to the rhythm of life
Shown in many compositions and colors so bright

Each resembles the versatility and wealth of the earth
Having the same nature within the state of the good
Smiling, laughing, shouting praise and singing to the

rhythm of life
The rejuvenating values within the core of the seed sown to rid strife

Soon pushed away to bear fruit and to meet the call to labor
Travels the bridge from here to there to a place called home
Tasted the purest flavors of this life during the earliest years
Are so embedded within the spirit of their position to cheer

The consistent recycling of nature's will
To generate the state of innocence and purity again and again
Will live forever, and within…

The children of the garden

The Stamp of Approval

Given the circumstances of our nature
One will choose to be — or not…
To be approved within the spirit of the self
Or, to linger in confusion to rot…

To choose to see the symbols in nature
To hear the many voices clear
Will free oneself from the ways of rote living
Yields the courage to live outside of fear

To know that one is on a worthy path
The state of a position sound
The greatest contribution to the song of harmony
To be heard in universe by all other states around

The lasting impression upon this energy field
A positive seed to sow
To encourage all to labor their unique direction
By wielding natures symbols of growth

The stamp of approval is nature's validation to each of us for being a creative symbol of life

The Leaf

Have you ever compared the veins in the hands of a man to the veins within a leaf?
So close of a reflection in both their texture and relief

The leaf and the hand alike
Are tender, yet hold the most powerful symbol of labor
To bear the sensitive vessels that deliver life's nurturing favor
To all of Mother Nature

To wonder…
What was God thinking when He made them so sensitive?
Reflects the fragile nature of their substance
And their willingness to labor through strife
After they coiled in the clay to join their energy
They took up the vessel to carry a life
Then gave to all of nature this chore
To deliver its substance for life evermore

The leaf is extended from the end of a branch
Connected to a tree that rises up from the dirt
To stand bold in the number of many having no perfect match
To spread its wealth across the surface of this great mother earth

The leaf delivers a very unique seed of life
Its true nature of laboring cannot be physically seen
Its vessel of breath still holds the energy it forms
Reflected in the offspring and through its texture

The wealthy color of green

A most precious gift of nurturing indeed
Soon pushed away from the bosom of its mother, to recreate a seed
To demonstrate its level of commitment to its labor
By providing the substance for all the earth to breathe

The hand is extended from the end of an arm
Connected to the trunk of man that was raised up from the dirt
To stand bold in the number of many having two, for a pair is a charm
To spread its wealth across the surface of this great mother earth

The hand delivers the physical symbols of labor
The true nature of laboring, sure to be seen as truth
Their vessels handle the energy they bred
Reflected in the offspring of their fruit's nature and relief
The wealthy color of blue

They wave before the universe to vouch where a man stands
After being pushed away from the bosom of the mother and away from the father's feet
The symbols of oath and willingness to labor
A seed of substance with hands to eat

Both the leaf and the hand carry the messages of vessels
To hold, handle, and deliver the substances of wealth

The Mystery Behind the Star

The mystery behind the star
To twinkle when it is far
To live among the register of…
The universal par

A symbol in nature that reflects the value of a jewel

To shine bright within the scheme of all lights around
Yet, to reflect and blend each color equally within its valuable makeup, definite and sound
Another twinkle in the makeup of the universal crown

So, take a closer look…
To see each shine…
The universal magistrate
Did just fine…

A symbol in nature that signifies the highest worth

Reflected to all such a glorious message…
A reflection of all the mother earth…
To look deeper and through the darkness afar

A symbol in nature that defines the mystery behind the star

The Fly

An act of energy and life…

Quick to survive the waves of strife

With wings…
To soar…
To suddenly and successfully employ a moving chore

To flee…
An attack…
To escape its enemy's "smack"

To leave…
The fright…
And rise above its sight

To save…
Itself…
From the crush of its life

A small symbol in nature that demonstrates survivability and an important act of flight

To Live Among Men

The greatest challenge of them all
To live among men…
With all his many makeups in nature
To figure out how to begin and win…

To measure life against nature's scale
To gain the weight to conquer or resist the many temptations waved
By pressing your life against the temperature gauge
Determined to avoid the wages of sin

The ways that we are raised are deeply rooted…
And this we cannot deny
So to learn to avoid the crush of any
Leap in faith to exercise the fly

The energy of a man does show his faith
Either the vessel of substance or the petrified state
To set your expectations is to know your weight
A compass by which to maneuver your acts of nature through any given state

We are all sensitive by nature to almost everything
And guarded by thorns we'll forever be
That's why it's so important to hear the many voices of nature
To set the captured free!

Where Do We Go From Here?

We're all in this state of nature together
To nurture our very position here
To learn the greatest lesson that we are in need of
one
another
To make life's song on this earth sound clear!

To sing as we travel through this beautiful garden
With the rhythm that will get us all through the storms
While enjoying all nature's fruit along the way
Sharing the substance of nurturing toward truth for all,
be born

We should all be traveling in harmony from here to
there and beyond this very land
Laboring the call to serve, share dinner and to cel-
ebrate our unified stand
Growing to understanding and appreciate of one
another during our individual travels - sowing while
knowing that we'll one day meet again
To receive the crown of life and our victory that is wait-
ing

For having labored to get to the distance so far
To continue to live together eternally and in universe
Someplace among the stars!

Twinkle...twinkle

The Sum of Two States

Mishap or Circumstance

What is the difference between the two?

Some food for thought…

Or

A fool that ought…

One, you control…
And the other controls you

The laws of nature have always been in motion
And to act against their cycle is to challenge nature's devotion to stand

A mishap is a situation consisting of elements of energy that have gone beyond control
For reasons of carelessness to leave the outcome to chance, and the lack of consideration given to the consequence of circumstance

A circumstance is a controlling position that clearly defines its fate
Delivering the limitations within the composition of its given nature and state

Fortunately, the consequence is joined with circumstance
And the mishap ties into the situation at hand
Giving man the choice to carry or not, the messages of Mother Nature's stance

To equate Mother Nature with a mishap isn't nearly a reasonable comparison
However, to pair a situation of man's nature with one of her substantial elements of energy offers a very clear explanation

To knowingly attempt any direct challenge of nature's authority to overrule
Clearly defines the composition of a weed transformed to fool

To deny the union of a mishap with a situation
And the nature of a circumstance fails to convince
Will eventually deliver Mother Nature's power to issue the appropriate consequence

So, to consider the situation at hand and to think before you act with any unknown natures
Will help you to avoid a mishap and the consequence from "its specific" cycles of circumstance

Leveling proof that nature ultimately controls the states, power, and choices of man by cycling its symbols of authority naturally

Do not underestimate the power of the Magistrate!
To be…or not to be
Symbols in Nature: Innocent and PURE

Two by Two

Two by two
That's where it all began
Continues to call us all
The creation of a pair to stand
A woman plus a man
Equates the sweetest treasure of nature to find
To share during this journey through the call to labor
The symbols required for enhancement, unity, and the balance of the mind

Two by two
A seed and a weed
Challenges the comparison of opposite ends
The measurement of life against nature's deed
Makes for traveling the path of one or the other — a race
To deliver with haste the lessons and payment for the cost of living
The wages required for either the act of taking or the act of giving
The final symbols dividing life's transformations and the composites of faces to trace

Two by two
Each creature upon the earth
Travels together across the bridge from here to there
The laboring of their own lives and their seed from birth
A number from which to begin the count of the many messages that are being delivered
Bred from the generations of nature's first two symbols
Holding the states, both Innocent and PURE

The Grasp of a Weed

While walking through my beautiful garden, an act of nature suddenly appeared. It seemed to have known the exact area to position itself to get my attention and to compliment all my fruit, so dear. I could not help but notice its stare and determination to stand out among the roots of my fruit. An awkward position to take, I thought to myself, still I allowed it to remain in place and began to study it for its beauty's sake.

As I continued to observe the makeup of its composition, it spread its beautiful blossoms to win my favor. Yet, I continued to observe its shell and the blossoms it bred at the first, and within a small period of time it became even more pleasing to my eyes. Needless to say, I began to nurture its composition in hopes to generate good seed to spread its uniquely arranged blossoms around my beautiful garden — to breed.

So with the labors to nurture and guide it to conform, I gave to it the substance of life from my veins and offered for it to hold its position within the makeup of my garden, just the same. Oh, to my surprise, I was so pleased to see that it accepted without delay to join right in to receive my nurturing and laboring deeds.

Days turned into weeks, and weeks turned into months. I continued to share my substance with this unique composition holding a beautiful blossom with the hope to soon harvest seed.

I labored and labored for the next couple of years not wanting to give up on the possibility of witnessing its transformation. So, I continued to give to it the same as all other fruit within my beautiful garden, the best substances of my energy and life.

One day, so unexpected, I noticed that most of the blossom was gone. The composition of its makeup was still in place; however, there was no seed to collect its state. I began to realize its slow nature to generate a seed, yet it was enormously resilient in maintaining its space to sit just around the roots and show its face.

The nature of this composition puzzled me. I recalled the numerous times that I had given to it my substance as I had given to all other fruit the same, and asked of it, "Why is it that you do not respond to my energy and life to have you generate a seed? I have allowed you to remain in place within my beautiful garden because you have such a beautiful blossom. I have nurtured you with my substance and have never known your name. Still, you just sit there and have not shared the same."

To my dismay, the composition finally responded after a few days, "I am here for you to help to adorn your most beautiful garden. I am not like any other. I'm different because I was raised to be this way. Please do not give up on me, for I am telling you the truth."

I replied, "But I've noticed your position to settle in to receive my substances of energy and life as been given to all my other fruit, and yet you've taken a position so close to only one root. Still, you've never borne a seed, never mind a fruit. Do you not see that you are puzzling me?"

"Yes, I do see what you have done for me, but please give me time. I will never disappoint you for being so fine to allow me to remain within your most beautiful garden of life for which you have sacrificed!"

"Well, I have been waiting for years for you to respond. I am now asking for you to give to me a more direct explanation for the position of your composition. I cannot afford to continue giving time to you neither can I allow you to hold this place or give to you my substance. Do you not see the level of my commitment and the sacrifices that I have made for you, to have you generate good seed and to share with me your fruit?"

The unique composition did not reply, so I began to remove it from my sight. I gathered every tool that I could find to collect its makeup and to relieve my mind. So I labored, to discard its traces by tossing the evidence of its composition away from my beautiful garden; although it wanted to stay.

By this time, I could not see myself giving in to this composition having such a vague position. So I removed it from my beautiful garden. I was too tired and very disappointed to learn that I had received no return for my labor yet, I was relieved to be rid of its unmotivated, unproductive and unidentified composition. It deceived me and nearly sucked the life out of me as it slowly damaged the fruit of my garden. I went on about my business to continue the labor of my garden's compromised and failing condition. I realized areas within my beautiful garden that sat very close to the unidentified composition had obviously suffered from the little substance and attention received over such a period of time. So close, but yet so far from expanding more unique blossoms within my beautiful garden. I was so focused on generating a seed from a composition that was only willing to receive.

Still puzzled, I often wondered about the nature of such a composition having a state that would only receive the substance of my energy and life while allowing me to suffer the burdens of laboring its strife. And even more, to have a blossom so beautiful which yet, would never generate a seed that I could collect to plant within my garden to breed. Meanwhile, I continued to labor within my beautiful garden to regain the original states of the fruit therein. Hoping to never have this situation happen again.

I began to give more attention to the areas of my beautiful garden that had endured the compromise of their beautiful state. How could I have lost my focus of the full state of my garden to give less of my substance and energy of life? Undoubtedly from my demanding sacrifice. I recalled the very position where this unidentified composition sat while taking notice to the root of my fruit's wavering petition. Low and behold, a reflection of this unproductive composition was in the same position.

So I dug around and beneath the root of my fruit. Only

to find this vein that did not look the same. And, as I remembered, this unidentified composition never told me its name. I knew that I did not care to revisit its unproductive state so I began to pull once again the evidence away. I pulled and I pulled until I became too exhausted in all my own compositional makeup; laboring to maintain my beautiful garden. I found that this vein was spread under the ground to surround all of the fruit around. I desperately pulled again with haste to avoid more losses of my harvest to waste, behooved to search for a similar face of its underlying and vaguely revealing compositional blossom to trace.

No place in sight, this vein was the only evidence that spread its attack beneath the ground and all around the roots of my fruit. It was very obvious to me by now; this underlying composition had been taking the nurturing substances away well beyond my true vision of it. I immediately grabbed my tools again and ran to the far end of the garden to verify the vein's position in full — to pull back the ground. And again, it was spread all around.

So I pulled and pulled some more until I became so frustrated, I lost my will to continue to till. I sat still, thinking…what should I do? I have worked so hard to labor my fruit and yet, I have found this aggressive vein around most all their roots. This unidentified composition never once generated a seed with all my attention given it and nurturing deeds. How could I have been so blind to allow my beautiful garden to become so consumed by such a composition, and for such time?

It showed its beautiful blossom and appeared to hold a face of truth. I was so hopeful that it would surely contribute to my creation of more beautiful fruit. I should have learned from its lack of laboring a seed to deliver the evidence beyond its word as proof. I must now define its face to prevent this tragedy from ever happening again within my garden, or within another. Therefore, I will give this blossom a name to prevent its grasp just the same. I will track its pattern of travel within my garden lapsed. I will establish its position, state and the level of the substances it eats. Its nature of travel will be determined to be underlying to never generate a seed, but breed aggressively to attack around and about the root of fruit within a beautiful garden. Its purpose takes away substances to deprive a fruit's nature and will to survive at best, to steal their will to thrive to the state that produces good seed. From this day forward, I will call this blossom a weed.

A symbol in nature that describes the grasp of weed…
An underlying message to set the captured free!

Within You

Each element within nature's nomenclature has been issued a definite position and form of identification by the universe. Each element is carefully categorized with such precision and arranged within nature by its known energy or the potential of energy held within its core makeup. Man has collected, studied, learned and composed many of the elements found within nature to reveal their intertwining and complex compositional makeup. Obviously, man has been successful to wield the very separate and purest states of energy from raw elements as each value was realized. Man explores the very elements of energy that he values within nature and labors faithfully to understand its true nature and to generate its purest form. Meanwhile, man will not search to collect elements of energy that he does not value.

The elements within nature have always been available to man, however, the value of the raw elements had to first be realized, reached, collected and finally transformed. Moreover, the energy possessed beneath the shell and within the core of raw elements has required man to labor to also categorize their values. Each value of energy therefore is arranged within a state among other energy similar to its form, thus allowing man to quickly and safely determine appropriate usage options. Man has gained payment for their great weight and unique mineral characteristics. The mineral usage has been maximized and man has become dependent on many of their energy to live and thrive. Likewise, the elements of natures within a man have always been available however he has not always realized the true values he possesses within his core. It is with good reason, I presume man would know after years of living upon the earth that "his true nature" is key for navigating life's transitions to wield the energy beneath his shell and within his core to find the purest form of his natural existence upon the earth. Yet, most men will not search and labor their core natures as faithfully to bring about such purifying transformations. The level of weight that a man applies to his personal gains, as well as losses, does determine the transformation that takes place within his core nature. Thus, the transformations that a man realizes will ultimately direct or redirect his attention. He will determine the position and the values he holds within any state to be a constant value within the nature of a state or he will labor to evolve into new positions. His nature in whole will be based on the value that he realizes through experience. The ability to categorize the values of all experience determines a man's ultimate state or rather state of mind. The enlightening gained allows man to push open the buds that surround his blossom to spread open his arms and to embrace the universe. He learns to value his life and freedom to choose to be or not. Moreover, he values the lives and freedoms of others to do the same. To be naked of nature's truth does leave a man void of his true "natural potentials."

Man, without a doubt, has been able to enhance many areas of life by employing the energy collected from nature. Likewise, man should consider the same potentials do exist within his natural and spiritual makeup. He should learn to improve his life through first developing a more optimistic outlook of self. Secondly, he should learn to utilize the pureness of his core values by employing the true potentials of his nature realized from experiences gained during life's various transitions. The balance of both bad and good experiences forces man to respond by categorizing his thoughts and behaviors within the value of either nature. Thus, the freedoms that man finds within his core are truly in his choice to value either experience as they both deliver elements of enlightenment. Enlightenment should change a man's energy or transform his state to become more pure, thus steering his direction of travel through life. The freedom of choice to develop a certain state of mind is ultimately the only freedom that man controls and will determine his pureness. Man does have the potential to absorb the impurities and purity transferred by others simply by allowing their influence to become transducers. The choice to filter the positions others hold and the type of energy they generate from the state of mind in which they live can help you categorize their values within your transformations. Your true and natural potential is within you and only you can deliver the purest forms of your uniqueness and values to labor for the enhancement of your life and the lives of others. The full nature of a man will never be completely known, however, knowing more of the truth, either way, allows leniency in understanding how to plan and explore advancements to improve life. A wise man collects, studies, learns and composes his findings to appreciate his raw shell. He quests to find the values within the core of his shell and labors within and outside of his beautiful garden to determine the values of his natures and the natures of others no matter what category the universe has placed them. Certainly, we can all agree that man has no valid reasons to doubt nature's positions for being so diverse or cause to deplore the very states that it allows man to hold a position upon the earth, whether he is wealthy or poor. For the life of a man is more valuable than any riches found in all the mineral of the earth. If a man does not find and refine the purity within his core (willing to be transformed) he starves his soul of the most valuable treasures of nature's will to have him live and thrive. Therefore, the positions of wealth and poverty are so intertwined within man the same as within the earth and in universe. A man's wealth is generated through his choice to hold a position, state of mind and value system for categorizing his life's transformations.

We all want to live and thrive, not just survive. Giving labor to the core of a seed equates to the truth in its nature. To labor for truth in understanding nature offers favor that gives the necessary relief to live and thrive. The laboring of balanced choice keeps man alive. We must labor so that all men can understand how to receive the substances necessary to refine a valuable position among man rather than have him be confined to a position that bounds him within a den. Any adverse positions and states among men aren't nearly enough to celebrate. We as the seed of the earth must look closer and deeper within our core and others in order to connect with nature's messages. Nature's voice teaches us how to truly live among the many compositions of mankind. The complex compositions of a man's nature are all found within the composition of all nature's states whether good or bad. Who is the man who does not hold all of nature's ways? All natures within nature are within you. We all have work to do…

These are the symbols that cycle in nature's voice.

The Ocean and the Sea

The ocean signals the motions for the cycles of a wave
Formed from the overload of its balance — its natural quest and state to save
Rolls vastly in on tide, the sand with the dirt and waste from the sea
Spills upon the shores from its adorned surface, willed to spread across the land to find its belly's relief

Forces all the earth's elements to see their variance to reposition when disturbed
Reveals the potential of fluctuating hands for man's nature when perturbed
The disposition to refigure its composition when such a forceful hand of nature is dealt
Delivers witnesses for such acts of occurrences for even the largest bodies that carry the colors and substances of wealth

The symbols that signal for man to realize his obligation to offer the necessary relief and balance to all bodies burdened with overload. The wave of the state for homelessness is a search for immediate help…

The Vein Network

To be a vein that gives the substances of energy and life…

Or…

…the other called a weed

The Belly of Nature: The Sponges, Breath and Liquid Veins of the Earth

Nature's belly holds wet, dry and invisible forms of symbols that are cycled through stages of time and age. Each delivers the transformations of its core to reflect outwardly for all to see its individual nature. The sponges, breath and liquid veins are bridged together to carry the energy and life that define the borders around the earth's surface and down through its core.

Its overall composition is the same as the tree reflecting the colors of wealth, both blue and green, branching out about the earth in so many sizes and forms, none being a perfect match. Each branch of energy holds a leaf with substance in meaning to take on the symbol of a weed or a seed. These two symbols do ultimately establish the challenge for all life forms to learn, divide and conquer to sustain life.

Although these leaves are bred separately, the challenge of selection through free choice remains ongoing and forces these two energies to mix and travel all stages of nature's belly. Each life form must learn to filter and absorb the nature of their differences to fall like leaves to collect around the root of its trunk.

To recognize the substance and message of the life energies within nature's belly is truly a remarkable sight. The intertwining of all substances is the inevitable commitment that nature in whole establishes in order to maintain the cycle of symbols that flow through her freely.

The belly of nature does deed all life forms the will to continually regenerate life from the breath of the leaves that is spread around its trunk. These are the branches from trees that reflect the symbols of innocence through their buds that blossom. The buds embrace and nurture the seeds before they are pushed away from the branches to initiate a new cycles of life. The first nature of the seeds that are released from the buds does hold some of the nature of the tree that bred them to first root in the ground upon which they fall. All seeds are recycled through nature by the issuing of a deed to feed or a deed to breed.

Again, seeds inevitably take their first root in their first ground, however, the nature of the core does determine a seed's will to remain or be repositioned by other natures around it. The belly of nature does take in all seeds, and yet, will recycle the waste after absorbing the nutrients from their substances. One cycle must consume some part of another in order to yield the relative values in its individual makeup to begin its transformations and will to survive life. These very cycles are intertwined within the flesh, blood and bones of men to yield the same will to generate and sustain life.

There are values in each man that are worthy to absorb regardless of the differences in his makeup. The many levels of substances and meanings possessed within each different body of man do contribute to the cycles of purification and rejuvenation within nature's belly. Man is a significantly powerful symbol of a seed whose life demonstrates the very same transformations to yield branches and buds that blossom to bear seeds. These seeds are nurtured and eventually pushed away to fall around the roots of the trunk that extended the branches that carried them. They too, take their own root among the nature of those sharing the same ground, yet the core does determine whether or not an individual seed has a strong enough will to choose substances that give life. A seed will maintain the full nature that was bred within it to breed the same, a seed or a weed, or deliver a new cycle of change.

The belly of nature filters the vast sponges, breath and veins by separating their forms, temperatures and movements. Each form demands its own attention by reflecting the seasons possessed within the energy cased beneath its shell. These seasons are the individual gradients and cycles of its life that projects the energy it possesses. Thus, the projected energy forms the symbol of either the weed or seed. The symbol of a weed that feeds upon a life or the symbol of a seed that feeds to breed life. The gradients of energy from each symbol create the earth's complex rainbow above and beneath the earth's horizon from the mixture of the vast number of shells clashing between stages of hot and cold. The elements of hot and cold define the barriers that exist between the stages of growth that each shell must break through in order to enter into either, the transitions of energy. The positions held during the transitions are constantly changing as each shell does fluctuate between barriers of choice for one reason or another. For man, the position and value each shell holds within nature's whole will generate a specific transformation of growth toward understanding the purpose of truth and his life. The ultimate purpose of nature's transitions, between hot and cold or a weed or a seed, carry man toward a direction of enlightenment to make better choices that should keep him grounded. The revelations that come from the wisdom and knowledge gained causes man to reflect upon his experiences and should enhance his ability to travel successfully through and around the many sponges, breath and liquid veins of nature's belly.

The energy generated from the sponges, breath and liquid veins are the reflections that are spread throughout the universe to create the symbol of a map. Land, air and water make up the trinity of nature's union to create the vessels of her belly mapped out to feed her seed of every kind. Sponges, breath and veins are vessels defined by their ability to hold and carry substances. The division of these three symbols is obvious, yet still equal to the one concept of traveling. Each vessel carries purposeful substances that hold meanings that should enlighten man to gain direction while traveling through all nature's transformations. Man should become inspired to find the purpose of the clashes experienced between transitions of his travel, "the will to live," while sharing the graces and relief offered through nature's tears.

The transference of all substances undoubtedly passes through each level within this trinity to purify and rejuvenate their positions and states to regenerate life for evermore. Each level preserves and stores substances of wealth for all creatures upon this the earth to eat and drink. All substances upon this earth are symbols and must be "transformed" to yield the most pure elements from within their makeup.

The full nature of this belly is unknown to man. Even the transformations witnessed by the eyes of man can be as unpredictable as nature's four seasons. Consequently, each energy will respond to the challenger of its will to live in very unique ways while traveling between dawn and dusk within the light or within the blind. All energy is given a position, direction and state to travel through all of nature's cycles. Take the opportunity to acknowledge the substances and meanings that are reflected around, through and within all of nature.

We are all a makeup of nature's trinity; the sponges, breath and liquid veins of nature's belly. We all reflect registers on the face of the navigating tool, the universal compass, and do point toward specific directions of travel through life's transitional seasons.

Think again…

Naturally "Driven"

The guidepost for interaction
Sows a seed or a weed
Encompasses nature's concision
To breed or to feed

Indwells each element of energy
And pervades its final composition
To deliver the breadth of living freely
...or the depth of slowly dying

The cycle of individuation
Each parcel of a course
Makes more sensible the messages
Retrieved from nature's voice

The symbols in nature consequently proclaim the effects of beliefs on internal and external states of relief and survivability.

Naturally...

The Eternal Rule

How many ways can one say "hot or cold?"

We are all standing on nature's scale and up against the temperature gauge, the measures of our response to the call to labor.

It's your choice...

The Laboring of Four Seasons

As with nature, the life of a man is seasonal. Winter, spring, summer and fall are the four seasons of nature as we know them. For man, the seasons are vastly complex and influenced by the four seasons of nature, the seasons of those who labor our seed from birth, and the seasons of those we encounter while traveling through life.

Change is quite evident when considering both the seasons of nature and man. Obviously, man expects nature's seasonal changes year after year and prepares for them accordingly; however, he would do well to consider the seasons of life and man's seasonal natures with the same vigilance. It would not be wise to say that man has no consideration for the changes that occur in day-to-day living. Man should consider giving more attention and substance to the nature and seasons of a man's life and the core of his soul throughout his life rather than wait until the very moment when his life is on the fall. Sadly enough, not even the nearing of death will initiate serious consideration for some men to alter the nature of their position and stand. This message is a wakeup call for each of us who truly cares to make a positive difference in the lives of others and for those of us who need to be rejuvenated to see the truth regarding man's existence and composition within nature. Ask yourself these questions while traveling (reading) through the four seasons of man; what is most important about a life and its laboring upon the earth? Considering that we all began with the core states of innocence and purity, where will we all end up? The frailty of life and laboring to live are forever among us. The four seasons of nature undoubtedly offer to man the formula for which to categorize the four seasons of travel that will be labored upon the earth through birth, life, age and death.

Winter is the first season of the year. With this season brings new life on earth. It's a time when a seed that has been embraced by the earth is settled into a place where it will take root to soon break the earth's crust to travel and bear its own seed. Likewise, the birth of a human being is a season of newness and hope to deliver a pure seed. Generated from the seeds of two that coiled, offers to it the same beginning of newness of life to create a reflection of itself by traveling into existence in the form of a symbol "shell" to live among the universe. Birthed by its mother, a child will travel to leave its first embrace to face the world. And, as this child was embraced and nurtured in the womb of its mother, it will continue to feed upon the nurturing and labor of its parents. The home is the place where it will be toiled to spring up to live as it was raised. It is most important to realize the impressions made at such a tender age. For these impressions will be the weeds that chasten them throughout their lives or the seed of hope that will carry them through their travel of the world. The first impression of newness offers the child a green seed possessing the substance needed to travel far in life.

The season of spring delivers the blossoms and fruit of all new seed bearing the most beautiful faces of nature, although not all new seed falls on the most fertile ground. The joys of living are now clearly before the eyes of children and the true nature of man's reflections appear vibrantly colorful. Children are inspired to believe that there is joy and hope beyond the canvas of the horizon waiting to be captured. The time of hope and dreams, and such their compositions, plan the laboring for a better life. Their outlook and excitement couldn't be more rejuvenating. The freedom to experience optimism, at its best, to see the world as a place where life is simply a choice to make to carry on the pureness of living life and the hope of bearing good fruit. It is the season of spring that a child will leap forward into the world to challenge the ground that nurtured its roots holding a determination to make its own way among the natures of men.

And given the time, the season of age soon brings the summer when the earth has become worn. The temperature is hot and the experiences from life's unexpected change begin to cause a disengagement and the perspective of the world in whole becomes broken; the outlook becomes distorted. Although rain with heavy dark clouds will occasionally fill the sky, the sun will yet reappear to dry "and clear up" the view. The true nature of life's seasons begin to sink in and the burdens to labor them diligently continues. With imperative alliance, man continues to complete the labors of this season only to realize that age is a benevolent sign that time is really of the essence. The questions of origination, position, state and destination seem to take precedence over the mortal labors at hand and the spiritual life is pressed against the temperature gauge – to stand. The weight and measure for both spiritual labors and life worth are aligned far beyond the earth to refine the position of his state.

The season of fall finally arrives, as man continues to look far beyond the canvas of the horizon to search for his true place among nature. His thought becomes more immortal as the inevitable spiritual awakening of his temporary existence upon the earth and the acknowledgement of death lingers around and about him. He is truly inspired to assess the distance he has traveled. The outlook on the world and all things of the world that once inspired man's shell to labor through nature's seasons becomes less important; rather, the core of the soul and its final place of rest, calls for immediate attention. Unfortunately, or shall I say, consequently, the fall season is the time when man morbidly considers himself a true part of nature as he accepts his fate. Ashes to ashes…dust to dust…

Most men know and are willing to acknowledge the energy of life greater than himself, transforming him, as he bears labors through not only the most beautiful seasons of life, moreover the roughest upon the earth. Each new day offers man the opportunity to make positive impressions upon the seasons of everyone's life. He should be reasonable enough to reflect on the first two states of innocence and purity and hold the truth for the wave of all men of every color and weight. They are of equal values just the same, however, the complex differences and seasonal changes that exist among men stems from the varying of roots planted within their natures, first held by the ground upon which they fell to root around a trunk to feed.

These revealing impressions and symbols in nature saying, "Lift up your brother and sisters. Show them humility and the way to labor…lest you leave one to fall, you have missed your call."

Help someone to labor their garden to succeed with generating good seed…for we are all eating of the same fruit to sustain our very life upon this earth and thereafter…

The Forgotten Seed

A sad reality of life is the reflection of the forgotten seeds that fall just short of a beautiful garden. These seeds are the children not given the appropriate nourishment by those who bred them or the seeds that were pushed too far outside the ground of a beautiful garden and into a bed of weeds. Either way, the forgotten seeds have been given less than the appropriate attention. The cycle of generating displaced and unattended seeds is a definite cause for all good seeds to labor.

Yes, the seed of a child does take root in the ground where it falls. Each seed will carry the burdens of laboring the weeds that surround its roots. If the ground around the seed is not toiled and seasoned with fertile substances, the chastened roots are forced to succumb to the grasps of the weeds that entangle them. Its core is therefore deprived and the vessel that is created around it reflects its core state. The weed depreciates the substances that nurture the seed's will to live and thrive, thus, the seed struggles to survive.

Other forgotten seeds are the symbols that were raised outside of a beautiful garden. They are the generations of seeds that were pushed too far away and without nurturing substances within the core of their nature to thrive; they struggle to survive. These seeds are not free to rejuvenate their souls. Their vessels too will carry the partially ripened fruit collected the buds from the branches that bred them. They were not allowed to live completely within the purity of the core states first given yet, tossed out to live among weeds.

The vessel that is formed among weeds is hindered and will travel a less productive state for a while. For the core of such a vessel is stressed to survive life's transitions to travel through additional storms of life to reach a beautiful garden. Still, the forgotten seeds know that their fruit must first fall outside of a beautiful garden uncollected (vessel), void the state of a truly enriched and settled mind (ground). They will carry good fruit a distance toward a beautiful garden until the weight and stress becomes overbearing and the destination appears unreachable. The vessel of the forgotten seed continues to hold the desire to carry the collected fruit the distance, but is bound by the encompassing of weeds. Forgotten seeds are without the relief necessary to maintain an enriched position toward reaching an enriched state. The forgotten seed searches for the relief to lighten its load. In other words, the very state that determines the capacity of good fruit that will be carried by the forgotten seed, stems from the reflection of the devouring natures possessed by the branches that gave to it a life. Thus, the forgotten seed struggles to maintain its position to feed from the level of substance that was bred into it by nature to produce.

All children carry the will to live within the freedoms they naturally possess within their core, being Innocent and PURE. Although Innocent and PURE, few unattended children will fully break the grasps of the weeds that chasten them. They strive to produce while carrying reflections from the path of life traveled before being pushed away. If children are not nurtured to stretch their arms to extend hands that can reach, grasp and hold the substances that will create productive life; will cause their core to become hardened. A state of existence that will be reflected from within the core of nature's whole, offspring living in a petrified state. Thus, the heart within the fruit of the forgotten seed will become less sweet, bitter to die. It will harden rapidly to dry and become heavy. It falls closer to the dust of the earth as a shriveled shell with no ability to sustain its weight, but is forced to drop to the earth to be recycled through the cycle of nature's cry.

The tears of children transform their state that has cracked like the mud. Their tears are hands waving their need for nurturing. Children all around the world continue to call out for someone to not just bear them, but to hear them and care to labor their needs to not just feed, but to breed. A child's need to belong to a beautiful garden goes far beyond the earliest years. The state of the outer shell, even in adults, permissively reveals the sign that indicates a definite need for the substances of wealth. Children all around the world continue to call out for someone to not just bear them, but to hear them and care to labor their needs to not just feed them, but to breed in them knowledge and the wisdom to thrive in life. The forgotten seeds should be harvested and repositioned within a beautiful garden by laborers to regenerate the true state of their core.

A symbol in nature that identifies the need for harvesting the seed of our children, to not only survive for a short while, but to thrive as they travel through life having a will to also labor the four seasons.

The Relief of Nature

As I arrived closer to the completion of this book, I found that I had been moved by the full collection of the messages. These messages have positively impressed upon me a long reflection of my life. I've realized that taking on this project has made me more aware of my own positions and states of existence within nature. I have grown more inspired.

My initial inspiration for writing this book was ever present and powerful, however, I experienced more revelations during the course of writing that were very challenging and enlightening. They too, became inspirations contributing to the development of this book.

Before I began writing, I set my goal to complete this book within seven to eight months. I found that my goal would require more of my core energy as I worked. I was comforted by the many inspirations that I continually experienced along the way. Somehow, I've known that this composition is unique.

Each phase of the book's development allowed me to generate new inspiration that reinforced the messages and enhanced my vision of their delivery. After all, I've trusted my inspirations would be meaningful and appreciated by readers. Therefore, I have lived within the content of this book for eight straight months. I worked rigorously to maintain my focus and balance by filtering daily living and relationships to enhance my inspirations. Honestly, trying to explain my dedication and inspirations to those who were closest to me was not so easy to do! However, I'm thankful that I had great supporters assisting me in one way or another, if nothing more than to listen to me as I filtered life during this time. Moreover, defraying acts of nature and the chastening of weeds were forever around and about me during this time. Still, I was determined to share these inspirations with the world.

The development of this composition proves that nature does show us favor and give us relief when substance and meaning are sought after from the complexities within our lives and those around us. Likewise, nature does allow us pain, even while laboring within a beautiful garden. The symbols of joy and pain as well as a seed or weed will forever be a part of nature's cycles. These are some of the natures that come with the sacrifice to labor and to sow good seed.

I would like to encourage you to continue to push forward and through all energy that may surround you. Please keep in mind that the true freedoms that you will experience in life are within you. Only you can travel through nature to rejuvenate your core. The rewards of laboring within the core of the self for substances of wealth deliver earned lessons from both the joy and pain however, sacrificing them for the good of others is much more rewarding to the soul. Laboring is one way nature offers to each of us the relief needed to live and thrive, not just survive. I have grown stronger and wiser while traveling through my beautiful garden. Parts of me have been purified as well as rejuvenated.

This is my personal testimony to the world expressing my hope for this book to be just as inspirational, rejuvenating and purifying for you. I trust that you will find some relief by realizing the symbols in nature and to hear the messages within her voice.

So does nature continue to cry…

A symbol in nature for understanding…"WHY?"

The Language of Nature

The universal echo of generative energy
The synthesis of the earth's multiplex symbols with the elements of eternity
The voluble cycles for the laboring seed to travel and endure
The position of praises that claims the state of being…
Innocent and PURE…

Speaks nature's voice…

The Face of a Messenger

The face of a messenger appears to us all
In one form of nature's energy or another
Bearing the same volition to hear the beckoned call

Both a seed and a weed are deemed to carry nature's voice called life
The natural polarization of each makeup will be their challenge to bear and sacrifice
To establish a compass of a light to focus within the darkness of strife

The face of a messenger presents the cycles of nature's symbols so intertwined
The deliverer of nature's messages who says to yield, and plot the direction of the mind
To force the balancing of the spirit within, and its compositional bind

To reflect a hand that waves in a direction of laboring the forgotten seed that's lost
The universal compass to guide the soul to a state that has earned its cost
For all matter upon this earth does hold the position and face of its choice

The Forest and the Wilderness

Many words can describe the two states of nature's gatherings — the garden filled with seeds (forest) or the garden filled with weeds (wilderness). Still, there is one ultimate power of travel that lives within understanding the mystery when taking positions in the makeup of their individual states, and should be echoed across the land.

A state is a territory in nature having definite boundaries, and a position is a temporary existence that is influenced by the forces of nature. However, both the forest and the wilderness are states of existence that hold a definite position. Man has referred to these two states, by their title, with one uniquely simple understanding of their case. The forest and the wilderness each hold life, yet the differences between the two are in the reflection of their face. The forest delivers the evidence of balance, beauty and the freedoms of nature's sight. The wilderness, on the other hand, delivers the evidence of uncontrolled elements, unsettling darkness and the worries of unseen strife.

To place a man in a position within either state is a challenge all its own, for him to learn to survive and to spare — the feeding of his most valued shell of natural flesh and bones. The natural quest he initiates to thrive will be increased by his will to think of how to survive among the many elements of each state. The common sense required to stay alive comes by the wisdom of knowing how to navigate — day by day. Take of that which is good for his seed to feed the life of his core by selecting only the elements that are known, leaving the others to nature's floor.

The forest is the edge of the state that holds a settled mind. The wilderness is the depths of its nature that chastens him to travel within the blind. The man who travels within the bounds of the wilderness is bound to trace the burdens of its face. And the one who knows to navigate around its edges is more likely to find the substances of wealth allowing him to save his case.

The compass of nature is a powerful tool to use to cross this very land. For nature is a universal tool of voices that registers man's ability to navigate safely the distance of life's journey — around the dark natures of man.

The symbols in nature directing man to travel the graces of the forest, bound to offer rest, and to avoid taking the route of the challenging wilderness — to gain one more day of a fruitful living, at best

Speaking with Substance

What in the world must a man do to have the wave of
his hands hold true?

Each man was born into a pre-established garden
— the existence of a state
Took root in the nature of the substances he was fed
— the very seed he ate

Delivered unto him the energy that influenced the
development of his initial composition
And soon to depart with the meat from the seed, and
the complex matters that reared his very face
To wave an individual establishment among some
preexisting territory, the quest to hold his very place

An order deeded the influences from other minerals of
the earth also carrying their own nature to stand
Required him to balance the minerals and the
symbols from home with the circumstance at hand

The gathering of the mineral and their circumstances
did reflect the values of the matters he'd retained.
The call for some investment of his labor and time to
restructure his recollection, just the same
Weighed desperately the substances of wealth he'd
been given to live and carry his own name

The result of his ability to waiver his acts of fortitude by
reflecting on his state of origination
Began his new evolution to carry his own acts of
reflection to light his path as he navigates his travel to
reach a new destination

To realize this great challenge and requirement to survive living among men
Taught him to travel within the sight of graces from the forest and away from bewildering bends

A symbol in nature describing a man's ultimate challenge as he learns to travel through life. He must learn to balance the weight of seed given from home to gain balance of the true value of seed waved by the hands of others

He must appreciate the daily graces from the life he survives, simply to navigate clearly through the challenge of differences in substances of nature found within and among men

The Final State of Reflection

Mirage

The mystery of the eyes that blend the radiant light projected from the sky into the path of travel, creating a symbol of the ocean's wave. Flashes before the sight of the traveler creates in the mind the magnificent merging roll of the earth's elements in truth, both wet and dry, while coming out of the blind!

A symbol in nature reflecting the unseen truth in understanding the power of unified energy.

The message of focus and recollection...

Shadow

The existence of a simple concept and composition
that man should understand…

Projects beside him the image of truth with the pres-
sure from a beam of a concentrated light
The powerful reinforcement of a symbol for any position
that travels through a state without sight

Identified by the wave of rays that carry a heavy weight
of wisdom held high above the head
Makes visible the one, unified, image of a body cre-
ated when two like composites are bred

To reveal the opposite state of positions for anybody
holding the light out to the side
Spreads its darkness farther into the path of all posi-
tions traveling within the blind

For the man who understands and carries the light
closer to his core
Will find the path of his travel to be much brighter than
before

A silhouette of a man should remind him of the need to
navigate with sight
A deliverer of the symbol in nature that magnifies the
magnificent power of light

The Nature of Friction

Have you ever been rubbed continuously the wrong way?

Certainly, the nature of friction is confrontation on the way…

It generates from a contradiction of composing motions of elements standing too close
Or, the back and forth of opposing energy and notion for the state of mind, at most

The fluster and combustion that breeds an imbalance in the composition of a state
Heavily weighted, its scaled positions will soon bear the excess of resistance and indigestible waste

Builds up to reach a limit before going into the topless state of overload
And, if not segregated or equalized in a timely manner, is more destined to explode!

Thus, creates a flame that blazes up and burns the composite of a face, decreased
The nature of friction is the spark that lights the fuel in its makeup and demands sudden release

The symbol in nature that illuminates the message to avoid standing too near — the opposite nature. A natural resistance to prevent the disintegrating of a complete state under pressure

The Flexibility of Nature

The force in nature holding a duty to accommodate all of nature's existence in whole
Leveling the constant fluctuation of the positions of her varied boundaries by states
To relieve the imbalance of overflow in her cycles to breed transitions of equal return
Always to travel in a forward motion while spinning its instruction and directions to learn

Generating a natural process of growth and a remedy for any case of trial and error
Minimizes the friction and shock from its inevitable resistance to change the core of its soul in nature
Yet, to fold and to offer the balance in the knowledge of nature's most weighted territories
To deliver a detour from the lifting of too much weight, and from the grinding revolutions of stress and undue worry

The revealing energy that gives warning before allowing nature's positions and states to fall much worse
A sign that signals the time to balance judgment and assist nature to simply take its course!

The flexibility of nature is sure to answer back with the most daring weight of resistance to force its challenger into a non-competitive match — to "SNAP"

A message from the symbol in nature that carries the definite weight of a circumstance as an effort to eliminate an overrule by the most unforgiving state of mishap

Sanity for Humanity

Such is the case for sanity...
Life's weight and balance scale for all of humanity!

The equalizer of all thoughts and actions
The composing of many positions to build a state from fractions

The tally of the parts does total to make a whole
With more or less the weight distributed from the collected travel to mold
Reflects the state of the seed that is planted within the spirit of nature's soul
Sanity for humanity balances the position of being courageous with the state of being bold!

Your current position and state of your existence is no guarantee for the future composition of your face
For, the forces of nature's cycle could easily shift the scale of equilibrium to suddenly lessen your weight

So, judge not the man with less the weight in body or in mind
Even when knowing the true position of his state, to have traveled so far within the blind
So close, but yet so far, to reach much deeper within his seed to the core to find
The means to pull him outside of the barriers of his navigating restrictions and dark confines

To sit petrified, within either cycle, to make no effort toward a positive difference within the state of such motionless travel
Obviously, going around and around and never coming

outside of such a state of mind to enter the known state of its visual gravel
Makes everyone a victim within the vacuum of the continuous evolution of struggle, bound within a controlled state — to twirl
The delivery of a definite position and consequence issued to all for allowing such a state of imbalance to exist, any place, within the world

A symbol in nature recommending a readjustment of the scale for humanity to offer relief to the imbalance of states weighing less
We are all responsible for eliminating and preventing the persisting of any positions and conditions that would allow such imbalances to exist

The state of insanity is the result of both overload and underweight conditions and cases that requires humanity to have some humility to reposition the weights that will truly balance everyone's state of existence

Any sane person will understand and agree that humanity has an obligation to balance the weight of all substances to deliver equality to all positions within its great state. A balanced state provides everyone with life's necessary symbols of relief.
Why should any of our brothers and sisters struggle alone to carry such a heavy load to live?

We must all contribute substances of wealth to the scale of humanity to balance the positions within its state to carry the true power of humility, and to reflect the weight of a willingness to give

Nature's Voice

Look closely…
Look deeper to see the wisdom within her face
The composite of the earth's elements positioned with the most magnificent grace
Aligned and arranged in universal array with many compositions of gleaming crystals, traces her very state
Held together and orchestrated by the majestic hands of all forms, her creation
The synchronized chime of unique symbols to signal the direction to a final destination
By the ringing of the messages from each cycle of her seasons rolled up in equal modulation
Spreads swiftly across its territories with many levels of explanations

The temperament of equality issues a scale to measure her vast number of positions and states
A reflection of each condition and the balancing of each soldiering weight

Listen…
Listen to her many positions and states cry out, "Hear their call to labor…"
Be willing to labor a call; and to bear good fruit earns equal favor
To claim, hold, and deliver substances of a wealthy flavor

"Assist her in the toiling of good seed to create a beautiful garden of cordiality
To establish a place for man to, once again, find his rest and to eat of all her fruit, so plenty"

Nature's voice…
The composing of one vessel of substance tunes the

universal veins of light in truth
To reflect a rainbow, lined in spectrum, with the wealthy colors of green and blue

Ride her waves as she navigates across the bridge, and through the darkest of storms
Compassed by the sight from the light of her crystals aligned and arranged in universal and magnificent forms

A signal…
Her symbol that waves a message — clear
Bred lessons for living within her boundaries and are very worthy for all to hear

To feed the hunger and to quench the thirst of the laborer who rests assured
To claim the rewards from the harvest of the fallen and forgotten seed, for sure

"Stand with assuredness during the travel to the eternal home. I'll get you there. Eat of the fruit that are given from the brothers and sisters traveling with you. Join in and sing the song of harmony! Rejoice in the grace of living within the states of their existence. Embrace the core of this journey called life. Hear my voice and know that you are never alone…"

The ultimate driving force of nature echoing cycles that circulate her substances of wealth in knowledge to deliver the wisdom to endure
Hear nature's voice…
Symbols in Nature: Innocent and PURE

Message from the Author

Again, I wrote this book as a result of being inspired by a homeless man. Realizing the state of his condition and the frailty of man's position to hold and maintain a productive state of existence, the lucidity of my thoughts compelled me to write of man's sensitive natures and in line with many of nature's positions and states as I view them. Certainly, the reading is subjective, creatively presented and open to personal interpretation. However, I am hopeful that most readers will appreciate my delivery and will be inspired to look deeper into nature's individual positions and states to retrieve the symbols and messages that echo in her voice.

The integration of man with nature is inevitably distinct; however, focusing on individual positions and states allows very unique comparisons of man's evolution and his quest to conquer his place and purpose among nature as well as the many complexities of positions and states of his mind, body and spirit.

I wish for readers to share with me this natural and soothing reading experience in effort to simplify the universally complex makeup of man and his will to survive and thrive while living within nature.

I am thankful for the personal experiences that have allowed me to observe nature, retrieve these symbols and messages, and the ability to generate the sensitivity and inspiration to deliver such a sublime reading composition for enjoyment, clarity and relief.

Once again, I would like to thank those of you who have been so kind to continue your support of my work.

Timothy J. Culver

The Guiding Symbols of Nature's Light

Symbolic References

Section I — Just A Few Thoughts

FREE FORM: THE CHOICE TO BE OR NOT TO BE

DISTRACTIONS OF SORTS: OVERWHELMING FEELINGS AND PESSIMISTIC VIEWS

INSPIRED BY NATURE: A CYCLE OF SYMBOLS IN NATURE CALLED FAITH

THE MIXTURE: BEGAN THE CYCLE OF SYMBOLS IN NATURE'S VOICE

THE FORCES OF NATURE: DESCRIBES THE CHALLENGE OF OUR DAILY WALK THROUGH LIFE AND NATURE

Section II — The Rules of Composition

SYMBOLS IN NATURE: YIELD TO THE SIGNS TO "HEAR" NATURE'S VOICE

INNOCENT AND PURE: A MOST VALUABLE STATE OF EXISTENCE — THE STATE FROM THE VERY BEGINNING

THE CALL TO LABOR: AN HONOR AND A PRECIOUS GIFT FOR LIFE ETERNAL

THE BRIDGE: THE VISION OF TRAVELING FROM HERE TO THERE...

AND THEY WERE NAKED: A REMINDER OF THE CALL TO LABOR — TO EARN BACK THE STATE OF PURE

The Waking Giant: He who wakes us and orchestrates our transformations toward purification

To Toil a Seed: confirms the acts of nature's symbols of miracles. To toil a seed and witness its revelation is a definite testimony for the power within nature. The symbol in nature for the cycle of giving to receive the most honorable blessing

The Veins of the Earth: provides all the earth elements the necessary substances of wealth to live and to thrive

The Carrier of Life: universal breath and energy life force

A Cycle: coming into the light and out of the blind

The Harvest: whatever is sown will be harvested

Nature's Tears: the symbol of rejuvenation given as purification

Nature's Symbol of Time: the symbol of evolution and growth

From Dawn to Dusk: the cycle of remembrance to meet the call to labor again and again

Nature's Symbol of a Back Breaker: the ant; a small symbol in nature that meets the call to labor

Pushed Away: required of each symbol in nature so that each may bear its own fruit: initiates the true growth experience

The Supreme Beam: a symbolic giant within the universe that humbles all of nature and nurturing

The Queen of Night: offers rest and thankfulness, reminding us all to get life right

The Genders of Nature: THE UNIFIED CHORE OF MAN AND WOMAN TO REPLENISH THE EARTH WITH GOOD SEED

Why Opposites Attract: ORDER TO MAINTAIN BALANCE; A NEGATIVE MAGNIFIES A POSITIVE

To Be Pure: ACCEPTANCE OF THE CLEANSING GRACE

Dust of the Earth: TRANSFORMS THE STATE OF IMPURITY INTO THE CYCLE OF PURIFICATION

Crystal of the Earth: A SYMBOL OF CALM AND UNITY

Reflections: A CYCLE OF TRANSFORMING LIFE THROUGH VEINS TO ALL OF EARTH'S CREATIONS

Flesh and Bones: THE SHELL THAT RECEIVES, CARRIES, SOWS AND REFLECTS THE LIGHT

Journey of a Lifetime: A CYCLE FOR LIVING WITHIN NATURE

To Be Transformed: CYCLES INTO THE STATE OF INNOCENT AND PURE FOR LIFE ETERNALLY

Nature's Scale: A SYMBOL OF MEASUREMENT AND DIRECTION FOR NATURE'S ELEMENTS THROUGH TIME

Temperature Gauge: READS HOT OR COLD — NOT IN BETWEEN

Spine: KEEPS MAN IN LINE WITH THE CALL TO LABOR

The Evolution of Motion: A NECESSITY FOR TRANSFORMATION OF STATES, POSITIONS AND PROGRESS

A Song of Harmony: A STATE, POSITION, OR SYMBOL OF THE EARTH BEING IN ONE ACCORD

Universe: DEFINES THE MAGNITUDE OF MAN'S SOUL

The Rainbow Effect: THE REFLECTION OF ONE ANOTHER; A REMINDER OF OPPORTUNITY TO CONQUER THIS LIFE WHILE CROSSING THE BRIDGE FROM HERE TO THERE

The Core of a Seed: FOUND IN ALL THE EARTH'S ELEMENTS HAVING LIFE, AND CARRIES THE MOST FERTILE POSITION FOR RECEIVING AND SUSTAINING LIFE

The Fertile Seed: CARRIES LIFE'S CORE OF LIGHT

The Hollow Seed: EMPTY, DARK, AND IN NEED OF LIGHT

Mind: PURPOSE AND LEADERSHIP

Heart: RECEIVES AND GIVES LIFE FROM A VEIN CARRYING SUBSTANCES OF WEALTH; REVEALS THE NEED FOR THE SUBSTANCES OF WEALTH WITHIN ITS CORE

Spirit: DELIVERS THE CYCLE OF SYMBOLS INTO NATURE'S EAR AND OUR VESSEL FOR HEARING THE CALL WHEN "THEY" ARE NEAR

Soul: SHALL MAKE KNOWN THE SEED IT HAS SOWN

The Gift of Giving: PRODUCT OF A GOOD SEED

The Gift of Receiving: PRODUCT OF RECEIVING GOOD SEED

To Quench your Thirst: RECEIVING THE SUBSTANCES FROM VEINS CARRYING THE WEALTH OF LIFE AND IS REQUIRED FOR PURIFICATION WHILE TRAVELING FROM HERE TO THERE.

To Feed your Hunger: PARTAKING OF THE FRUIT TO REJUVENATE THE FLESH AND BONES THROUGH THE RECEIVING OF THE WEALTHY SUBSTANCES WHILE TRAVELING FROM HERE TO THERE.

To Rest: MEASURING THE LABORS, FRUIT AND STATE OF THE SOUL

To Move a Mountain: CARRYING THE LIGHT OF FAITH DURING THE TIMES OF COLD AND DARKNESS WHILE ENDURING THE LABORS OF A STEEP AND HEAVY LOAD

The Beauty of a Garden: THE PRODUCT OF SEED THAT IS NO LONGER IN THE DARK, NAKED AND BLIND!

The Crown of Life: A STATE OF STANDING BOLD, AND YET THE MOST HUMBLE — AS A MOUNTAIN

Section III — Lasting Impressions

I can recall...: A CHILDHOOD MEMORY...

Explanation Territory: MAN'S TEMPORARY EXISTENCE AND LIVING BY GRACE

Butterfly: THE GENTLE NATURE OF BOTH STATES INNOCENCE AND PURITY, AND THE EVOLUTIONS OF FREEDOMS THEY WILL FOREVER HOLD AND DELIVER

Deeply Rooted: THE WAYS THAT WE ARE RAISED ARE DEEP WITHIN THE CORE OF OUR NATURE

Deny Me Not...: THE NATURAL EXPLORATION OF A NEWLY FOUND STATE...

Eclipse: ALIGNMENT, BALANCE AND UNITY

The Colors of Wealth: BOTH GREEN AND BLUE CARRIES AND DELIVERS LIFE'S SUBSTANCES OF WEALTH TO ALL THE EARTH ELEMENTS

The Softness of a Rose Petal: BRINGS TO LIGHT THE TRUE STATE OF BEAUTY AND THE PRICE FOR LIVING

On that Day: THE DAY THAT ONE IS FREED TO LIVE ETERNALLY

Overflowing: CELEBRATION OF UNITY AND WEALTH

Petrified: MOVE THROUGH LIFE WITHOUT ALLOWING HARDSHIPS TO HARDEN THE CORE OF THE HEART

Discretion: UTILIZING WISDOM WHILE MANEUVERING THROUGH LIFE

Expectations: ESTABLISHING A DEFINITE DIRECTION TOWARD A DESTINATION

NATURE: AN EXISTENCE OF ENERGY

ACTS OF NATURE: ACTS OF MAN...POSITIONS AND STATES

SENSITIVE BY NATURE: LOOK CLOSER — LOOK DEEPER

CRUSTY MUD: FRAGILITY OF STATES DURING TRANSITION

MINERAL OF THE EARTH: REFLECTS THE LABORING APPROACH REQUIRED OF MAN

THE ELEMENT OF ENERGY: DEPICTS MAN'S INFLUENCES ON EVOLUTION

TO WALK ON WATER: OFFERS A PASS TO GET THROUGH THE ROUGHEST OF STORMS

THE CHILDREN OF THE GARDEN: GENERATES THE STATE OF INNOCENCE AND PURITY AGAIN, AND AGAIN

THE STAMP OF APPROVAL: NATURE'S VALIDATION TO EACH OF US FOR BEING A CREATIVE SYMBOL OF LIFE

THE LEAF: BOTH THE LEAF AND THE HAND CARRY THE MESSAGES OF VESSELS; TO HOLD, HANDLE AND DELIVER THE SUBSTANCES OF WEALTH; THE SYMBOLS OF TRUTH, OATH AND WILLINGNESS TO LABOR

THE MYSTERY BEHIND THE STAR: SIGNIFIES THE HIGHEST WORTH AND THE REWARD FOR LABORING UPON THE EARTH

THE FLY: A SMALL SYMBOL IN NATURE THAT DEMONSTRATES SURVIVABILITY, AND AN IMPORTANT ACT OF FLIGHT

TO LIVE AMONG MEN: MAN'S GREATEST CHALLENGE

WHERE DO WE GO FROM HERE?: THE TRAVEL...

Section IV — The Sum of Two States

MISHAP OR CIRCUMSTANCE: FOOD FOR THOUGHT...

TWO BY TWO: THE SYMBOLS REQUIRED FOR ENHANCEMENT,

UNITY, AND THE BALANCE OF THE MIND; THE FINAL SYMBOLS DIVIDING LIFE'S TRANSFORMATIONS AND THE COMPOSITES OF FACES TO TRACE; BRED FROM THE GENERATIONS OF NATURE'S FIRST TWO SYMBOLS; HOLDING THE SUM OF TWO STATES — BOTH INNOCENT AND PURE

The Grasp of a Weed: DESCRIBES THE GRASP OF WEED. AN UNDERLYING MESSAGE TO SET THE CAPTURED FREE!

Within You: THE COMPLEX COMPOSITIONS OF A MAN'S NATURE ARE ALL FOUND WITHIN THE COMPOSITION OF ALL NATURE'S STATES TO REFLECT ONE OF THE SAME POSITIONS WHEN CHALLENGED.

The Ocean and the Sea: SIGNALS FOR MAN TO REALIZE HIS OBLIGATION TO OFFER THE NECESSARY RELIEF AND BALANCE TO ALL BODIES BURDENED WITH OVERLOAD; THE WAVE OF THE STATE FOR HOMELESSNESS IS A SEARCH FOR IMMEDIATE HELP...

The Vein Network: WITH ANY GIVEN POSITIONS OR STATES MAN WILL BE ONE OR THE OTHER...

The Belly of Nature: THE TRIPOD AND APPLICATION OF THE UNIVERSAL COMPASS...

Naturally "Driven": CONSEQUENTLY PROCLAIM THE EFFECTS OF BELIEFS ON INTERNAL AND EXTERNAL STATES OF SURVIVABILITY AND RELIEF

The Eternal Rule: CHOOSE...

The Laboring of Four Seasons: SYMBOLS IN NATURE THAT SAY, "LIFT UP YOUR BROTHERS AND SISTERS WHEN THEY TRIP ON A WEED. SHOW THEM THE WAY TO LABOR...LEST YOU LEAVE ONE TO FALL, YOU HAVE MISSED YOUR CALL."

The Forgotten Seed: IDENTIFIES THE NEED FOR HARVESTING THE SEED OF OUR CHILDREN, TO NOT ONLY

SURVIVE FOR A WHILE, BUT TO THRIVE AS THEY TRAVEL THROUGH LIFE HAVING A WILL TO ALSO LABOR THE FOUR SEASONS

The Relief of Nature: SO DOES NATURE CONTINUE TO CRY FOR UNDERSTANDING... "WHY?"

The Language of Nature: SPEAKS NATURE'S VOICE...

The Face of a Messenger: ALL MATTER UPON THIS EARTH DOES HOLD THE POSITION AND FACE OF ITS CHOICE

The Forest and the Wilderness: ECHO FOR MAN TO TRAVEL THE GRACES OF THE FOREST, BOUND TO OFFER REST, AND TO AVOID TAKING THE ROUTE OF THE CHALLENGING WILDERNESS TO GAIN ONE MORE DAY OF A FRUITFUL LIVING, AT BEST

Speaking with Substance: DESCRIBES MAN'S ULTIMATE CHALLENGE TO LEARN HOW TO TRAVEL THROUGH LIFE HOLDING THE BALANCED WEIGHT OF THE SEED RECEIVED FROM HOME AND THE TRUE VALUES OF SEED RECEIVED FROM OTHERS. APPRECIATING THE DAILY GRACES FROM THE LIFE HE SURVIVES, SIMPLY TO NAVIGATE CLEARLY THROUGH THE CHALLENGES OF DIFFERENCES IN SUBSTANCES OF NATURE FOUND WITHIN AND AMONG MEN

Section V —The Final State of Reflection

Mirage: REFLECTING THE UNSEEN TRUTH IN UNDERSTANDING THE POWER OF UNIFIED ENERGY; MESSAGE OF FOCUS AND RECOLLECTION

Shadow: A SILHOUETTE OF A MAN SHOULD REMIND HIM OF THE NEED TO NAVIGATE WITH SIGHT; DELIVERER OF THE SYMBOL IN NATURE THAT MAGNIFIES THE MAGNIFICENT POWER OF LIGHT

The Nature of Friction: illuminates the message to avoid a stand too near — the opposite nature. A natural resistance, the disintegrating of a complete state under pressure

The Flexibility of Nature: a message from the symbol in nature that carries the definite weight of a circumstance as an effort to eliminate an overrule by the most unforgiving state of mishap

Sanity for Humanity: recommends a readjustment of the scale for humanity to offer relief to the imbalance of states weighing less; the universal responsibility to eliminate and prevent the persisting of any conditions that would allow for any less position to exist

Nature's Voice: "Stand with assuredness during the travel to the eternal home — hear my voice and know that you are never alone..." The ultimate force of nature echoing cycles that circulate her substances of wealth in knowledge to deliver the wisdom to endure life upon the earth

Hear nature's voice...

Symbols in Nature: Innocent and PURE

Global Weather Alert: The importance of urgency and knowing the travel itinerary

Nature in Whole: The choice to be or not to be a seed or a weed does not eliminate the value of messages driven by the whole of nature to offer direction for living.

Crystal Columns

GLOBAL WEATHER ALERT
STAR TRAVEL GUIDE

Weather Station: The Universal Base of Eternal Rule

Application Methods: Truth Assessments

Alert Condition: Worse Case Scenarios

Category Rank: Natural Disaster

Projection: Star travelers should expect various natures of dark clouds to appear on occasion during the travel from here to there.

Potential Index: Frequent / Scattered / High to Low Flux

Safety Requirements: The frequent changing of the weather conditions will require faith, environmental awareness, a purposeful destination, a clear understanding of symbols in nature, knowledge of the travel itinerary and courageous navigating.

Announcement: This is a global weather alert!
Please…
May I have your attention?
This is a global announcement!
Star travelers should be aware of the following weather conditions…
Whether unexpected or vaguely anticipated…

The projected forecast report indicates some dark clouds may lead to a natural disaster – and is considered a "major state of weather"
Brought on by the sharp strikes of forced friction…
The clashing of collected differences…
The dark stems within the intertwining of varying natures
Fused together…
To create gyrations of turmoil…
Made up to whirl unpredictable energy – the untraceable cycle of confusion…

Its cycle of energy "in whole" does deem to be boss
Wearing many faces and chases to chasten a star traveler…at any cost
It searches for hostages…
Holding a potential to burrow its way over most positions - standing within its path
Pushing through stable states as a conjugated mass
Extending its darkness of lies toward the direction of lights
To deliver disruption and to deflect all segments of sight
Basically…
It's a broad sweep of the globe – to brush over the truth
The effort to collect all clear vision from any star traveler – traveling "eternal bound!"

It appears to make its way in the form of unthinkable cases

Carrying waves of cold thoughts and poor behaviors
If by chance…the initial clouds formed within the travel area are not dark enough – a build up of negative energy will be created by some part of its mass to cast the shadow of its dark nature – the pattern of darkness reflected
To generate more negative energy from the surrounding winds…
And as time allows – these winds will cause more damaging blows
Until the clouds become too dark for clear travel to continue
Please, whatever you do – be aware of these signs as you travel…

Flashing signals may appear and reflect many forms of "light resistance" as travelers push their way through darkened areas
Some flashes may signal – "temporarily lost" or "wrong way"
Other flashes may only go so far – and the signs will read "dead end"
These are such extreme weather flashes that indicate a natural disaster could be approaching!

Its scattered clouds will typically layout a maze - from all known directions
Specifying less than operable weather conditions
– depressing the course of travel to create low moods
- allowing very little travel information or visibility to

reach star travelers
In fact, if the resistance persists, moods could possibly reach an all time low – a very challenging state to travel through during this time of the season, so please, be careful…
Watch out for the sudden placements of new challenges – the stirring around of signals that seem to be more strategic in nature
The symbols that halts all rational movement – at least for a while
A definite indication that a natural disaster is making efforts to capture and hold travelers in their places
To be barricaded by its underlying nature – "intimidating energy with gusting streaks of rolling fright"
Set up to mark a position from which to attack the star traveler's most stable state and stand
With invisible weapons filled with the ammunition of strong high winds; pointed and pushed on by the undercurrents through the barrels from obscurely positioned angles – creates more thrusts of piercing winds to come in from the blind
Although these tactics may seem subtle - at the first
These are very engaging weather conditions…
Be prepared - they will eventually get worse…
Acting to reposition the traveler's "state of mind"
To force a fight – forcing sudden chaos and unplanned sacrifices
Unnecessary…preoccupations – course paving with the holes and gravel of unworthy investigations
To confine all light within a den of binding borders that only allows travel within the restraints of its darkness

- being limited to the path of "not knowing…"
Just long enough to tear down and remove all known columns of courage…
And to rip up the brightest paths before the eyes of traveling friends…
To block the through traffic and to defeat the will of good natured travelers and their good intentions…

A natural disaster is prone to be very unforgiving
Its an out of control traveler – all its own
It stands aloof…
Still, it's the primary creator of unsettling disturbances – among many
Stirring up many forms of winds…
Developing more patches of scattered darkness – from a distance
To form stages of clouded judgment – the furious efforts twirled to defeat and hide the truth
The signals of weariness and hidden agendas
Marking star travelers to whistle their steps from gaining knowledge and understanding; only to misguide their steps into more darkness – will sit and listen to the wind blowing and faithfully count each whistle blown…to point out to each undercurrent known
Do not underestimate the low whistles in the wind – the scattered pollution
Spreads only the harshness of worlds – the packed barrels of rolling dilutions
Performs many vague acts of concern only to mislead with drastic illusions – a shady travel guide

Acting to take away the substance necessary for gaining "logic" in reasoning…
Feeding from all energy that opposes the star traveler and waves on the subtle and unnoticed back drafts that will occasionally head around its bends – the bushels of thorns raveled within the stems of straw being carried by the same wind
A mess of pessimistic reflections flashed in an optimistic direction
Trust me, trying to reason with a heap of negativity - you just can't win
Take the position that paralyzes its rejections and objections…
Just know the power of reflection – for no other plan or strategy will map out a clearer direction of travel toward the ways to completely avoid all forces of their wind
Reflection will help you to quickly readjust your internal perspective…
You may have to abandon your worldly goods along with their unjustified opinions…
When both the time and direction of travel are of the greatest concerns
And you've found yourself in this state of blasted trash
You'll be required to make a sudden decision - to book a speedy ticket
Hopefully one way…
To find a new direction toward clear and purposeful travel…
You must look within your spirit to find your ticket…
The "on site verification" that you've secured your light;

a guaranteed guide arm offering the most secure travel reservation – by placing the travel ticket right in your hands and stamped with the fine print that reads "trust your inner spirit and hear the messages offered by natures rewarding symbols"
Confirmation that you've received the appropriate travel itinerary…
And the exact time you're required to depart!
Wave before departure - to inform a friend…
To establish another column to strengthen the bridge
Because a natural disaster is one big complicated face of nature
And each crystal that shines for truth will create a clearer picture
You'll definitely want to learn to draw its composite
– and share them with star travelers as best you can!
Although the true natures of its character aren't at all
- fully comprehendible
It, no doubt, should always be considered - a very dangerous storm!

The movement of a natural disaster is rigidly complex "zigging just to zag" – a nagging wag - a definite sign of its unstable index
It holds a position and stance of pessimism – a reflection of its internal make up
A petrified case…
A case that explodes to release the hardness – the fillings of distorted stories told many times over…
Planting hollow seeds with tiny, but sharp fragments of

its hardened and cracked shell of doubt to project into your soul – with every given opportunity
Not a safe case to pack and carry – try optimism instead; a lighter case filled with wealthy substances and wears a more flexible handle…
Bear in mind…the power of choice!
Do not choose a case weighing less than optimism because it will only weigh you down

A natural disaster can attack from any direction - at any given time
So be advised of this seasonal weather forecast…
Reflecting the extreme acts of nature that defrays travel expectations
Or rather, attempts to eliminate the star traveler's combination with the Light – a mixture that yields wisdom from the "guaranteed travel guide" who grants the enlightenment of the power within your spirit - cases your eyes and your ears to see and to hear the insight of its nature and the will necessary to know the course layout and the direction through all dark areas of life

The aftermath of a natural disaster leaves its solemn effects
Torn up homes, lives destroyed, lives lost - all irreparable
The extreme laboring to pay for the costs – seems unbearable
Great needs fallen to the side – hails the razors of the blind
Simply to cut down the star travelers stride…

The unfortunate side of nature that gains a boost from salvaging the rubble

But don't give up…keep pushing forward
Perseverance is worth saving for tomorrow!
Even with such enormous repair costs…
Surviving requires a recollected mind and the endurance to live day-by-day
Whether permanently or temporarily blinded…
There will always be extended hell to pay…
However, the direction and distance already traveled – could yield an even clearer detection of a natural disaster's future patterns of harm
The reflections offering potential deflections
If you are certain that a natural disaster is heading your way…
Just know to move completely away from the areas subject to its attack and the falling residue

Hopefully, you can get a head start as it travels through surrounding territories
Do not allow it to reach the borders of your position and state – move away quickly because there will be no easier escape!
You can never be too sure which way it will turn with the notion to chase you down
Increasing the pressure to break a crest in the star of your crown – to deliver the burdens of its wrath
Evolved from the horrific energy it built up to wave its claims while traveling unattended – an out of control

cycle of confusion that continually repeats itself

It continues to whirl the winds wherever it grazes to build up the tension – collecting more garbage just to make a fuss "to mention"
Wanting the slightest retaliation – the only way to justify the thrill of degradation with the hounding hope to defeat a star traveler's quest to be saved
Stealing the good wealth of their nature by sabotaging both character and name
These are definite signs that should not be ignored...

Provoking disturbances and challenging good will since the beginning of time – a natural disaster is still determined...
To prevent star travelers from making a positive difference – and the swaying of others the same!
The sure sign of a prowler from the darkest pit – spreading the darkness of "ignorance!"
The darkness of ignorance will be extended into the path of star traveler's to fog up their sight with collected smog and to spread trash across as many positions and states as possible.

A natural disaster is an irrational force pushing unreasonable and unwarranted levels of harmful energy, negative stigmas and criticisms; a busy body for all the wrong reasons. Its mission is to rid mental balance and optimistic navigation to prevent star travelers from reaching their destinations and from passing on the light to bystanders seeking clear directions.

A natural disaster tosses about ill natures that yield the detours leading to the dead ends of darkness in the flesh and spirit. It's the very darkness that compasses the horizon of the universe to hide the beauty of nature. The counterproductive acts of spreading malicious information to distort, mislead, or misrepresented the positions and states of natures holding and carrying the sensitive substances of wealth and good intentions; can only be described as the most tragic energies of nature.

If these worse case scenarios seem harsh, then I've done well to make my point regarding the natures of both man and the earth. Man must understand that all our natures contribute to both the light of hope and the groping along in darkness since the beginning of time. Our ability to grow in understanding rests on the columns of bridged support being given one for the other. Man should be more willing to give support rather than allow his existence within nature to become disastrously insensitive to others because of the complexities of differences found within the makeup of men. Each man spread across the earth is a column and a laborer of a hard pillar bearing unique positions, states and natures. Nature requires man to learn appreciation for the worthy service each column holds and carries regardless of the applied weight across the bridge. Each nut, bolt and screw has a chore to tender - not only to build the bridge, but to give to it the strength to stand through life's storms to thrive forever.

Men are independently different and yet, all men are the same in nature holding and carrying the will to thrive in life; not just survive. Man has been tasked to labor the earth and its many natures to not only give and maintain the life of his natural flesh and bones, but to rejuvenate and purify his spirit. One thing is certain; nature will be here when we've all traveled beyond the flesh to be recycled back into the dirt and dust of the earth that binds all men to reflections and eternity in one form of a vein or another. We must embrace and encourage one another with our veins to remedy our flesh and spiritual ailments through time and age with constant reinforcement of both individual and unified laboring and worth. Even the ant with its small size delivers the powerful messages of both independent and unified laboring through the seasons with purpose, courage and motivation while holding up the spirit of a back breaker. We should care for our own if by chance one of us falls. The ant is wise enough to know that this common gesture of offering relief should be shared among all. We must turn back to nature to gain a clearer perspective on just how far we've traveled within the world to preserve mankind instead of allowing the chastening of the worldly goods and vanities that keeps man traveling in the blind.

Should the acts of nature described herein this forecast be categorized as separate states holding and carrying unequal positions "overloaded with undue stress?" " Should each position be combined to establish one state reflecting one bridge that's in need of repair? I consider the travel through life a "universal (global) state of emergency" requiring courageous laborers to meet the call to labor for equality to not only refine the spirit to shine as a crystal column in the makeup of the bridge, but to know the value of holding and carrying individual weight within the makeup of the whole to deliver its full strength. If too many columns within one state are ignored to eventually collapse will leave the complete bridge compromised. Either way, each independent position within each state is a network of veins spreading some place across the globe to bridge mankind with both the knowledge and wisdom of how to best live among different natures or to tear down columns of men with the darkness of ignorance while traveling through her four seasons.

A symbol in nature describing the importance of "urgency" and "knowing the travel itinerary."

This global weather alert provides a "first aid kit" containing the substances of knowledge that can deflate dark clouds, break high winds and block out the negatively projected energy and its residue encountered while traveling. The instructions inside the kit recommends that you carry it at all times knowing that it's an optimistic and secure case. And remember, regardless of the path you are traveling to reach home – you will find the substances contained to be more potent for navigating the dark natures of life. You will always want to first apply the topical solution of graces found in nature's tears to release the strife and to prevent the hardening of the core beneath your shell. There's no better relief for medicating the bruises and wounds inflicted by the sharp strikes of nature's dark stems as you travel from here to there.

This book is a global weather alert! Please review this report as required whether a natural disaster is anticipated or approaches unexpectedly. Just keep looking up and reaching higher with time and age and you will always see the light pointed toward your destination! No, not one man is perfect but we all should strive and be more willing to appreciate the unique differences and substances of wealth that we each offer toward living together in a harmonious world. Writing this book is another step forward in my stride toward home through continuous self-improvement, maintaining a worthy service to mankind and an effort to encourage others to do the same regardless of life's challenges. I'm offering what I can of my substances of wealth collected along my journey. I am leaning toward the Light with faith knowing that my laboring is not in vain, but a vein holding and carrying the life to make clear my crystal column within the bridge; to help build, strengthen and brighten the path toward home.

Twinkle...twinkle wherever you are!

Making It Personal 4U Productions Inc. Products and Services

Corporate Mission Statement

• The mission of Making It Personal 4 U Productions, Inc. embraces the creative spirit of others by promoting the arts in education and lifestyle through scholarships, shared information and unique support services on a global level.

Corporate Theme

• Embracing Your Creative Spirit

EYCS: A Global Perspective on the Arts Magazine

• A Unique and Informative Professional Arts Magazine

• Offers opportunities for professional artists such as visual artists, theater and performing artists, musicians, dancers, published authors, gallery owners, educators, institutions, community leaders and others to publish and promote their work, ideas, scheduled arts events and other information.

• View MIP4U Productions, Inc. Web site at *www.makingitpersonal4u.com* for more details.

EYCS Arts Scholarships

• Generated through sales of books, products, private or public sponsors and donations.

• Offered to competitive students seriously pursuing careers in the arts

• Graduating high school students and current post-secondary art students

- Recipients are selected from submitted portfolios and overall professional presentation.
- View MIP4U Productions, Inc. Web site at *www.makingitpersonal4u.com* for donation options

EYCS Cancer Foundation

- Offers alternative support to the families and victims of cancer
- Provides financial support for the purchase of medications and other special needs
- Supports other not-for-profit organizations supporting this cause
- View MIP4U Productions, Inc. Web site at *www.makingitpersonal4u.com* for donation options

Advertisement Options

- Offer businesses, educational institutions, art museums, art galleries and individual professionals affordable advertising options within the *Embracing Your Creative Spirit: A Global Perspective on the Arts Magazine*

MIP4U Productions, Inc. Gifts

- View corporate Web site for produce pricing and shipping details at *www.makingitpersonal4u.com*
- Mail orders accepted

Promotion of New Authors

- Promotional services for published authors
- For service details and pricing, view corporate Web site at *www.makingitpersonal4u.com*

Sponsors

- Sponsorship of Art Scholarships and Cancer Foundation
- View *www.makingitpersonal4u.com* for details

Volunteer

- Professional volunteer for portfolio assessment
- View *www.makingitpersonal4u.com* for details

Ordering books:

··· All major bookstores online ···

Making It Personal 4 U Productions, Inc. corporate Web site *www.makingitpersonal4u.com*

Email
AuthorMIP4U@aol.com

Trafford Publishing
www.trafford.com

Mail Orders:

View book prices and shipping costs on the MIP4U Productions, Inc. Web site
Send official money orders ONLY
Include legible shipping address
Bulk order and pricing details available
C/O Making It Personal 4 U Productions, Inc.
P.O. Box 7690
Port St. Lucie, FL 34985

Reader Feedback:

Readers are welcomed and encouraged to share their inspirations in the forum within the MIP4U Productions, Inc. Web site at *www.makingitpersonal4u.com.*

Next Publication

The author's third book, *Faces: Compositions of Races* will be released in 2008.

Access the MIP4U Productions, Inc. Web site at www.*makingitpersonal4u.com* to read excerpts for this book and other published works

SPARKLING CREDITS

Jerry Plantz

Acclaimed public speaker, author and poet of patriotism. Author of *I Held the Flag Today*, one of the most popular patriotic poems in the country.

Author of two books:

I Held the Flag Today: Words of Patriotism

More Words of Patriotism

Web site: *www.Thepatrioticpoet.com*

Email: *poetusa@swbell.net*

The author resides in Lee's Summit, Mo.

***** A VERY SPECIAL THANKS *****

Marc D. Baldwin, Ph.D.

Edit 911 Editing Service

www.edit911.com

Denise Justice

Denise Justice Gallery

Original Fine Art

www.denisejusticegallery.com

Barbara J. Hightower

Instructor of Art, Retired

Joan "Slevan" Tucci

Freelance Writer

Ann Elizabeth Jackman, Ph.D.

AAA Compliance Specialist

West Area Administration

Palm Beach County School District, Florida

Clif Desmond

Web hosting and marketing

Arlisa LaShay Culver Felton, MAEd

Literacy Teacher

Douglas County Schools, Georgia

and

Irie D. Culver

My dear mother

for your continued support from the very beginning of my journey

Copyright © 2007 Timothy J. Culver
Making It Personal 4 U Productions, Inc.

NATURE IN WHOLE

We are all veins of the earth carrying substances of wealth
We are all connected far beyond our differences dealt
We are all miracles of life so intertwined
To labor in unity the core of nature's soul be sublime!

Let us all strive to reclaim the power from the states we were first given
Let us all conquer our position within the state of our nature — so vastly built and driven
Let us all fair the distance home by resting on one another, the symbols of columns given us for life to endure
For our nature in whole will forever call us all back to our origin, the states of Innocent and PURE

Timothy J. Culver

Copyright © 2007 Timothy J. Culver
Making It Personal 4 U Productions, Inc.

MIP4U Productions, Inc.

Please copy, complete and mail in the card below if you are interested in joining the mailing list to receive our *free quarterly newsletter* via email or postal mail

Embracing Your Creative Spirit: A Global Perspective on the Arts Magazine
Please visit (*www.makingitpersonal4u.com*) to learn how to subscribe or participate

----

(Please complete this subscription card entirely)

Check ____ Yes, please add me to your email list
Check ____ Yes, please add me to your postal list

Today's Date ____ / ____ / ____
Day/ Month / Year

Name ....
Last, First, Middle (Print)

____
(Full Name Signature)

Business or Institution ______________________________________

Date of Birth Day_____ Month_____ Year________ Male_____ Female_____

Mailing Address ______________________________________
Street / P.O. Box (Print) - Newsletters will be mailed to this address

____
City, State

____
Zip Code

Home Telephone(____)- ______________________________ Optional

Work Telephone (____)- ______________________________ Optional

Facsimile (____)- ______________________________ Optional

Mobile Phone (____)- ______________________________ Optional

Email Address ______________________________ Required

Mail this information card to:
Making It Personal 4 U Production, Inc.
C/O EYCS Newsletter Subscription
P.O. Box 7690 Port St. Lucie, Florida 34985

THANK YOU

If I had stayed down on the ground after my first trip over the vein of a weed, or the many weeds encountered thereafter, I would never have traveled this far nor grown mature enough to receive and deliver this unique blessing. Therefore, my advice to you is to get up each time you fall, stay encouraged regardless of what you have, and know that no one other than God will ever know where you're going and for what purpose, until you get there.

Timothy J. Culver

Copyright © 2007 Timothy J. Culver
Making It Personal 4 U Productions, Inc.

www.ingramcontent.com/pod-product-compliance
Ingram Content Group UK Ltd.
Pitfield, Milton Keynes, MK11 3LW, UK
UKHW041847190726
13854UKWH00002B/764

9 781425 108779